THE ILLUSTRATED HISTORY OF
THE ARMY AIR CORPS

HISTORY

AOP formed	10 August 1940 from Forward Observation Post (RA) into D Flight	
AAC formed	21 December 1941 (to administer PARA, SAS, and GPR)	
GPR formed	24 February 1942	
AAC dissolved	1950 (PARA and GPR absorbed in to infantry, retaining cap badges)	
AAC reformed	1 September 1957 (from AOP and GPR)	

Glider Pilot Regiment and Army Air Corps Operations

Europe

Norway	Op Freshman	19 November 1942
Sicily	Op Ladbroke	9/10 July 1943
Sicily	Op Fustian	13/14 July 1943
Bosnia & Herzegovina	Op Bunghole	19 February 1944
N France	Op Titanic	5/6 June 1944
N France	Op Tonga/Mallard/Deadstick	5/6 June 1944
S France	Op Dingson 35A	5 August 1944
S France	Op Dragoon	15 August 1944
Holland	Op Market Garden	19-26 September 1944
Greece	Op Manna	13/14 October 1944
Germany	Op Varsity	24 March 1945
Cyprus	Op Lucky Alphonse & Sparrowhawk	1955 - 1957 - 1959
N Ireland	Op Banner	1969 - 1 August 2007
Balkans	Op Grapple/Hamden/Oculus	1993 - 2007
Kosovo	Op Guardian (Joint)	11 June 1999 - November 1999

Rest of the World

Malaysia	Op Firedog/Malaysian Emergency	1946 - 1957
Korea	Korean War	1950 - 1953
Suez	Op Musketeer (Joint)	1951 - 1954
Brunei	Op Ale - Brunei Emergency	1962
Borneo	Op Ale - Borneo Emergency	1962 - 1966
Aden/Radfan	Op Nutcracker	February 1964 - 1967
Rhodesia	Op Agila	November 1979
Falklands	Op Corporate	2 April - 14 June 1982
Kuwait	Op Granby	December 1990 - 1992
Sierra Leone	Op Barras	10 September 2000
Afghanistan	Op Fingal	6 February 2002 - 20 June 2002
Iraq	Op Telic	2003
Afghanistan	Op Herrick	2006

THE ILLUSTRATED HISTORY OF

THE ARMY AIR CORPS

WRITTEN BY
ROD GREEN

First published in the UK in 2008 by
The Army Air Corps
Middle Wallop
Stockbridge
Hampshire
SO20 8DY

ISBN 978-0-9557814-0-7

10987654321

Printed and bound by Printer Portuguesa, Portugal

Design, typesetting and print management by Design 23, London.

Photographs by kind permission of the Museum of Army Flying
and the Army Air Corps.
Photograph on pages 142-143 by kind permission of Paul Goddard.
Photographs on pages 136–137, 159 (top), 170 (top),
180 (top and bottom), 187 (top left and top right),
188 (top left and top right) © Crown Copyright, images from
www.defenceimages.mod.uk.

Image of the Future Lynx courtesy of AgustaWestland.

Bibliography
The following works have proved invaluable in researching
this book:

The Army in the Air by General Sir Anthony Farrar-Hockley
(Alan Sutton Publishing/Army Air Corps, 1994)
The Savage Wars of Peace by Charles Allan (Michael Joseph, 1990)
Women at War by Nigel Fountain (Michael O'Mara Books, 2002)
The Joker by Pete Scholey (André Deutsch, 1999)
WWII The People's Story by Nigel Fountain (Michael O'Mara
Books, 2003)
Everyman At War edited by C. B. Purdom (London,1930)

Acknowledgements
Many thanks to all of the AAC personnel past and present who
agreed to be interviewed for this book. Thanks must also go to
Giles Penfound, Rick Dawson and Lynda Horton at the AAC
Media Centre who were enormously helpful when it came to
finding photographs as was Pam Woods at the Defence Image
Database and Geoff Russell at AgustaWestland. Many thanks to
Stuart McKean from Lynx Sports Management for helping to
coordinate the project. Special thanks to Colonel David Turner,
COS DAAvn, for helping to make it all happen.

Finally, we are enormously grateful to Derek Armitage and the
staff and volunteers at the Museum of Army Flying for their help
and guidance, and for providing access to their vast archive of
RFC, AOP, GPR, AAC and other general material relating to the
history of military aviation. This book would not have been
possible without the assistance of the museum and the
generosity of all of those who have donated photographs and
other material to the museum's archives.

CONTENTS

CLARENCE HOUSE

The Army Air Corps, the air arm of the British Army, has existed for just 50 years. However, the roots of Army flying go back as far as 1878 when, following earlier experiments into aerial observation, the first Balloon Equipment Store was formed at the Royal Engineers Depot at Woolwich. Looking back, we can now appreciate that this initial tentative step was to trigger a dramatic series of events which would see the rapid development of military aviation. In less than 100 years the Army has witnessed unprecedented progress, from the first powered flight of British Army Aeroplane No 1 in 1908 to the current large scale use of highly sophisticated and computerized aircraft and helicopters supporting military operations at every level.

The story of the Army Air Corps is a tale of passion, determination and vision. It is as much a record of aviation adventure as it is military history. At its heart is a record of duty and service that is second to none, and it is clear that the potent force that is the Army Air Corps of today has been built by men and women of courage and conviction. Current demands on the Army Air Corps are as great as they have ever been and I can only salute the officers and soldiers who continue to serve with great courage, tenacity and the utmost professionalism. The spirit of those who proudly wear the light blue beret not only echoes that of the early aviation pioneers, but also the character and determination of their predecessors in the Air Observation Post Squadrons and the Glider Pilot Regiment who served with such distinction during the Second World War.

As Colonel-in-Chief of the Army Air Corps, I am enormously proud of such an outstandingly effective military force that now sits firmly at the heart of the British Army. This splendid book brings to life a remarkable story of exceptional people and is a truly fitting tribute to mark the Army Air Corps' Golden Jubilee.

INTRODUCTION
COLONEL DAVID TURNER
CHIEF OF STAFF, DIRECTORATE OF ARMY AVIATION

F ifty years is but a brief moment in the annals of British Military History – a period that for many would be considered inconsequential. However, to the modern Army Air Corps, the aviation arm of the British Army, the past half-century represents a lifetime of achievement and an era during which men and women of great character, courage and conviction have worked tirelessly to create a force that has grown in both size and capability to become a key combat element of the Army's order of battle. It is a remarkable period of discovery, innovation and the exploitation of cutting edge technology. In many ways the history of the Army Air Corps is a reflection of the extraordinarily rapid advancement in aeronautical technology, but to those of us who have been part of this journey, it is as much about people and commitment as it is about equipment and aircraft.

This Illustrated History marks the Army Air Corps' Golden Jubilee by looking back at the key developments, events and decisions that have shaped Army aviation to be one of the British Army's most potent war-fighting forces. On 1 September 1957, the Army took control of a handful of ageing observation and light liaison aircraft from the RAF and the modern Army Air Corps was born. Support was provided on an ad hoc basis by the Royal Electrical and Mechanical Engineers and the Royal Army Ordnance Corps, while pilots were drawn from across the Army but largely from the Royal Artillery and survivors of the recently disbanded Glider Pilot Regiment. From this inauspicious start we chart the increasing reliance on helicopters - initially as observation platforms but progressively, over the fifty year timeframe, becoming highly effective offensive weapon systems.

The Army Air Corps story would not be complete without reference to the origins of Army flying and the earliest military flying experiments of the 19th Century. This early history has done much to define the character of Army aviation and the attack helicopter units of today take great pride in their association with the illustrious and celebrated pioneers of yesteryear. A superbly illustrated account, this book truly captures the essence of what it was like to be part of one of the most active, exciting and challenging military endeavours spanning the 20th Century.

'A'G.I. Thimbles.

Die Forged Nickel
Steel Ring.
Internal Diameter 2.2"
External Diameter 3.5"

'B'G.I.Thimble

'B' Rope Strop
300'm long.

Nº 4 Toggle.

300

'B' Rope Strop
300'm long.

'B'G.I. Thimble.

CHAPTER ONE
TAKING TO THE SKIES
1878 – 1918

The Army Air Corps has been providing the British Army with 'eyes in the sky', airborne transport and an aerial strike force for the last half-century, developing tactics, techniques, equipment and skills among the men and women of the Corps that have made it a military unit in which any soldier can say he or she has been proud to serve. The story of British Army flying, however, goes back much further than the founding of the Air Corps in 1957. The first British trials of equipment that could give battlefield commanders the undeniable benefit of being able to assess the situation on the ground from a vantage point high in the air were carried out not fifty but almost one hundred and fifty years ago.

For as long as men have gone into battle, military men have recognised the advantages that come with command of the high ground. From a hillside above the battlefield, commanders could observe both the enemy's and their own troop movements. From the high ground they were better able to direct their strategic resources, be it a detachment of cavalry, a phalanx of archers or a battery of field guns. From around the fourteenth century, when firearms began to be used in large numbers, much of the battlefield could, of course, be obscured by smoke. The discharge of thousands of muskets or rifles combined with the great clouds of smoke produced by both sides' artillery could make it impossible to see what was happening at ground level and almost as difficult to appreciate the ebb and flow of the battle even from the high ground.

Hiding your troops or cavalry from observers on a hillside became something of an art. Ditches and gulleys, woods and other hills were used to conceal forces held in reserve, ready to be brought into play when the commander decided the time was right. As ever in battle, the timing of strategic manoeuvres was crucial and to be able to make such judgements, you needed the best intelligence available. Observation

from the high ground could give you that, but what if you were left without such an advantage, or there was simply no high ground? A partial solution to that dilemma came in the late eighteenth century.

Although there are claims that a Portuguese inventor had come up with the idea some years before, the Montgolfier Brothers are generally accepted as having devised the first successful hot-air balloons in 1782. Joseph Montgolfier is said to have been inspired by watching washing drying over a fire billowing upwards on clouds of rising smoke. While he originally thought that it was the smoke that caused the washing to rise, Joseph and his brother, Jacques-Etienne, eventually realised that warm air was the real lifting agent and that warm air captured inside a large balloon could lift a man into the air. Following a number of trials, they demonstrated the lifting power of their creation at the royal palace of Versailles in 1783 when they released a balloon carrying a sheep, a duck and a rooster in its basket. The flight, watched by King Louis XVI and

RIGHT: A BALLOON BEING DEPLOYED WITH THE EXPEDITIONARY FORCE ON THE MARCH TO TOFREK IN 1885.

Queen Marie-Antoinette, lasted just eight minutes, reaching an altitude of around 1500 feet and travelling about 2 miles. The animals survived their ordeal unharmed.

The success of the Montgolfiers encouraged swift developments in balloon technology that led to the use of different types of fabric coverings and the use of hydrogen as a lifting agent. In 1785 a hydrogen balloon crossed the English Channel piloted by an American, Dr John Jeffries, who was serving as a doctor in the British Army. He was accompanied by French balloonist Jean-Pierre Blanchard, who had previously made an historic solo flight from Paris to Meudon in 1784.

Military strategists were, by now, closely following the achievements of the balloonists both in free flight and tethered ascents. The French Aerostatic Corps was formed in 1794 and was first deployed against the Austrian Army at the Battle of Fleurus that same year. The French were victorious and the corps' commander, Dr Jean Marie Joseph Coutelle was pleased to report that: '. . . I was able to distinguish infantry, cavalry, artillery, their movement and, in general, their numbers.'

Aerial observation had become a part of modern warfare for the first time.

ABOVE: AN OBSERVATION BALLOON IS LAUNCHED AT LADYSMITH IN 1900.

Balloons were also used on the other side of the Atlantic to great effect during the American Civil War. The Union Army Balloon Corps was first assigned to map-making duties but was used for observation during the Battle of Bull Run in 1861 and later impressed General W. F. Smith by ascending to an altitude from where they could direct artillery on to a Confederate camp. The general said: 'the signals from the balloon have enabled my gunners to hit with a fine degree of accuracy an unseen and dispersed target area.'

The Balloon Corps, although essentially civilian contractors, also established a hugely important military precedent when they flew observation balloons from a converted barge on the Potomac – the world's first aircraft carrier. The Confederate Army also tried their hand at ballooning but with somewhat less success. They did not have access to all of the materials and resources enjoyed by their northern rivals and were at one point reduced to using dressmaking silk to build their balloons.

While many commanders still looked upon the use of balloons as something of a novelty, others regarded them as an important development in military technology. The use of balloons in warfare was not, however, really a new thing at all. In the Far East, the Chinese had been experimenting with balloons and kites for centuries before the Europeans and Americans fell upon the idea of military aeronautics. Having pioneered the invention of paper, the Chinese quickly discovered that a paper envelope filled with hot air would rise. This phenomenon was seen at first as an entertaining whimsy, a toy with which youngsters could amuse themselves, sending small paper balloons sailing into the air with tiny fire baskets suspended below them. They burst into flames before they climbed very high. But there is some evidence to indicate that the

ABOVE: PREPARING 'GOLDBEATER'S SKIN' IN GLYCERINE AND WATER FOR THE MANUFACTURE OF BALLOON FABRIC IN 1894.

military used such balloons for signalling. Kites were also an important element of military technology in China up to 3,000 years ago. They were used for signalling and for observation and even, by the time of the Chu-Han War of 203–202 BC, in psychological warfare. General Zhang Liang ordered his troops to fly large kites high above the fog-bound enemy lines. Strapped into the kites were small children with flutes who played tunes from the enemy homeland. When the eerie music floated down out of the fog, the soldiers became both frightened and homesick. They are said to have immediately deserted their posts to head home without ever engaging in combat.

While they may not have been aware of the exploits of the ancient Chinese, the British had certainly been alerted to the success of balloon deployments by the French and the Americans. By 1862 two officers in the Royal Engineers, Captains G. E. Grover and F. Beaumont, were actively campaigning for the establishment of a balloon detachment and in 1863 experiments in aerial observation were conducted at Aldershot. Despite the perseverance of the enthusiastic officers, it was decided that the expense of taking balloons to war, coupled with the technical difficulties, made them impractical. The main technical objections were that there was no way of effectively producing hydrogen in the field and the materials available for the balloon envelope were not durable enough.

By 1878, when Captain H. P. Lee of the Royal Engineers and

Captain J. L. B. Templer of the King's Royal Rifle Corps Militia established a Balloon Equipment Store at the Royal Engineers' depot at Woolwich, the hydrogen and balloon skin problems were close to being solved. Templer, who was a schoolmaster and an experienced balloonist, was initially employed at a rate of 10 shillings a day to provide ballooning instruction for Royal Engineers' officers. He was soon to accept a regular commission with the Engineers, however, becoming Chief Instructor of the Balloon School and Factory. In this capacity, the now Major Templer helped to develop a process for producing hydrogen that involved the use of zinc and sulphuric acid. Previously, the gas had been manufactured by passing superheated steam over iron filings in a furnace, not something that was easily achievable should balloons ever be sent on operations. Templer also pioneered the use of compressors to store the hydrogen under pressure in steel canisters, allowing a balloon to be inflated almost anywhere, while his experiments with the balloon envelopes led to the adoption of 'goldbeaters' skin'. The material was actually a membrane that formed part of the gut of an ox and had been traditionally used in the production of gold leaf. It was impervious to hydrogen and, although difficult to work with, the perfect material for his balloons.

The Balloon Factory moved to the Royal Engineers' base at Chatham in 1882 where, underfunded and undermanned, Templer continued to train his team of instructors, scientists, carpenters, blacksmiths, fitters and riggers. They were belatedly ordered to deploy with General Wolesley's forces in Egypt that year, arriving too late to be of any help, then a detachment was ordered to Bechuanaland in 1884. Templer's resources were then stretched to the limit when he was asked to supply another unit to deploy in the Sudan.

In February 1885, a balloon detachment was sent to the Red Sea port of Suakin in north-eastern Sudan to accompany the expeditionary force commanded by General Sir Gerald Graham. The detachment was led by Templer and comprised Lieutenant Mackenzie, RE, plus eight non-commissioned officers and sappers. With them they took three balloons, their baskets and rigging, signalling apparatus, searchlights, a small gasworks and pumps for producing and compressing hydrogen, and 120 8-foot-long, steel gas cylinders, each of which weighed around 75 lb. The lighter-than-air contraptions certainly did not travel light.

The balloons were used as aerial observation posts, with

ABOVE: A BETA POWERED DIRIGIBLE ALONGSIDE A TETHERED OBSERVATION BALLOON OUTSIDE ONE OF THE FARNBOROUGH HANGARS IN 1909.

15

1878–1918

Lieutenant Mackenzie spending seven hours on duty in the basket as one of the balloons was towed behind a wagon in a convoy on a march from Suakin to Tofrek. Colonel Edwards, CRE at Suakin, commented: 'On the 25th March, when the balloon was able to accompany the convoy, the men derived the greatest confidence from it, as they knew that they could not be surprised, and the convoy itself could move much faster and more freely, only making occasional halts to close up.'

Edwards, however, resented having to second some of his own Royal Engineers to the balloon detachment when it became abundantly clear that Major Templer had far too few men adequately to deploy even one balloon. The experiences in South Africa and in Sudan showed that, if balloons were to be used for reconnaissance and observation, a detachment would need three times the manpower available. In other words, to put one, or at most two, men in the air required a ground crew of at least twenty-eight. From the very beginning, the 'pyramid' team familiar to everyone in today's AAC had been established, but the team at the base of the pyramid putting a balloon crew in the air outnumbered today's Apache crew by four-to-one. Refuelling and re-arming an Apache in the field requires a ground crew of just seven!

The fledgling aviators had not proved their worth to all of the commanders under whom they served in the field. The abundance of manpower required by the balloon sections, along with the problems encountered in transporting their equipment only served to sharpen the scepticism shown by some commanders about the usefulness of any intelligence gathered by balloon observers.

As late as 1908, in responding to a request from Chief of the

'. . . WHEN THE BALLOON WAS ABLE TO ACCOMPANY THE CONVOY, THE MEN DERIVED THE GREATEST CONFIDENCE FROM IT, AS THEY KNEW THAT THEY COULD NOT BE SURPRISED . . .'

Imperial General Staff Sir William Nicholson for their views on 'the practical utility of captive balloons in war', many senior officers expressed their misgivings about the quality of reports received from aerial observation. General Sir John French wrote: 'I can quote no instance of my having been furnished with information of any importance from the captive balloons. I found that the most misleading information had, in many instances, been given. Teams dragging firewood had been represented as batteries of heavy guns; cattle had been reported as masses of mounted troops; concentrations had been announced where no

out of Chatham, which was used for training, rented from him by the War Office. This situation was resolved in 1890 when the War Office was finally persuaded to establish the Balloon Section as a permanent unit of the Corps of Royal Engineers and massive changes were put in motion. The entire balloon operation moved from Chatham to Aldershot where special facilities, including a huge balloon hangar, were constructed. Experiments in aerial photography and the training of air observers continued, with Royal Engineer balloons participating in manoeuvres and artillery shoots, the Balloon Section establishing itself as an indispensable

ABOVE: ROYAL ENGINEERS GROUND CREW MANHANDLING THE BULKY *NULLI SECUNDUS* IN 1907.

concentration had ever taken place, and in no case, on the other hand, am I aware that any information of the slightest military value was ever gained from this source.'

While there were many who supported the idea of military aviation, its detractors had formed their opinions during the African campaigns and when the balloon sections returned to the UK they found funding from the War Office increasingly difficult to come by. The balloonists had outgrown the premises at Chatham, and Templer bought some land himself at Lidsing, about five miles

element of the military establishment. At the outbreak of the Boer War in 1899, three sections were despatched to South Africa and a fourth was sent to China in August 1900 to support the International Relief Force during the Boxers' siege of the foreign embassy district in Peking. The balloonists were no longer regarded as any kind of short-term novelty unit, but there remained a fundamental problem with their equipment.

Balloons could function perfectly well as observation platforms if properly tethered and held steady by an experienced ground crew. They could even function in free flight, every observer now being trained to control a balloon under such conditions, mainly in case of an emergency. Balloons were still next to useless, however, if there was a strong wind. Balloons of different shapes, elongated into sausages or more streamlined 'fish' shapes, to try to retain stability in high winds, were designed with limited success. A tethered balloon remained uncontrollable in high winds. A free-flying balloon would, of course, go wherever the wind blew it. What was needed was a flying machine better able to cope with adverse wind conditions.

One answer appeared to be to use a contraption that actually relied on the wind to get into the air – a kite. In 1903, Lieutenant-

ABOVE: AN INTREPID CREW MEMBER ATTEMPTS TO TRANSFER FROM A DELTA AIRSHIP TO A SPEEDING LOCOMOTIVE.

Colonel John Capper, Royal Engineers, took command of the Balloon Section, instigating a number of significant changes. Under Capper, officers and men served a four- or five-year tour with the Balloon Section rather than the previous two to three years, making better use of their experience and training. Capper also increased the number of Royal Artillery officers training as aerial observers and introduced new systems for air-to-ground signalling. But Capper also had the foresight to realise that the advances achieved by the Wright brothers and others in the development of powered aircraft would eventually make the balloon obsolete. In 1906 he appointed an American, Samuel F Cody, to develop kites – basically tethered hang-gliders – capable of

carrying a man aloft as an aerial observer.

Cody was, essentially, a showman. His real name was Cowdery but he took the name Cody as a young man out of respect for the famous Buffalo Bill Cody. Just like Buffalo Bill, Samuel Cody toured America with his own Wild West show, which he brought to Europe in 1890. Cody had long held an interest in kites, the story being that a Chinese cook he had met as a teenager on a cattle drive had shown him how to build what would now be termed 'stunt' kites. It was a short step from mastering kite flying to building a kite big enough to support a man, some of which Cody demonstrated at Aldershot in 1905. A year later Cody was a British Army Kite Instructor, the Royal Engineers having placed orders for several Cody War Kites and formed two Kite Sections. But Cody's interest in aviation extended far beyond kites. The Wright brothers had flown a powered aircraft at Kitty Hawk in December 1903. Lieutenant Colonel Capper had visited them there in 1904. Both Cody and Capper saw the aeroplane as the way ahead.

Officially, the British Army was uninterested in aeroplanes, preferring the more conventional technology of the emerging airship. Alarmed by the development of the German Zeppelin, the British Government had allocated resources to fund the building of British powered dirigibles and in 1907 Cody was involved in the completion of the *Nulli Secundus*, Britain's first airship. Capper and Cody flew the ship from the new Balloon Factory base at Farnborough to London in October of that year, circling St Paul's. But, in the face of an 18 mph headwind, they did not have the power to make it home, crash-landing at Crystal Palace. The machine had to be dismantled, to be rebuilt back at Farnborough as *Nulli Secundus II*. Although the instability of *Nulli Secundus* was to make it unreliable, other more successful airships were to follow including the *Beta*, *Beta 2*, *Delta* and *Epsilon*.

Unofficially, the army encouraged Cody to pursue his ambition of achieving powered flight in an aeroplane. Developments in engine technology meant that it was now possible, just as it was in a dirigible, to equip an airframe with an engine light enough and powerful enough to achieve the forward speed required to provide

17

1878 – 1918

ABOVE: SAMUEL CODY AT THE CONTROLS OF HIS BRITISH ARMY
AEROPLANE NO. 1 IN 1908.

RIGHT: IN 1911 A LEBAUDY AIRSHIP PURCHASED FROM FRANCE WITH
FUNDS RAISED BY THE *MORNING POST* NEWSPAPER WAS DESTROYED
DURING A TEST FLIGHT AT FARNBOROUGH.

the air flow over the wing that would induce lift. Cody flew an
unmanned powered glider and began work on his own full-sized
aeroplane design, the completion of which was ultimately funded
by the army. His Army Aeroplane No. 1 was completed in 1908 and
tested over a series of 'hops' at Farnborough that culminated in a
flight of 1390 feet in October. The aircraft crashed while turning,
but this is regarded as the first official flight of a heavier than air
machine in the United Kingdom. Cody went on to win many

aviation prizes, more powerful engines allowing him to fly larger and faster aeroplanes. Tragically he was killed along with his passenger while trying out his latest float plane in 1913.

As the fascination with aviation grew, so too did the disenchantment of many of the Royal Engineers officers attached to the Balloon and Kite Sections. Messing about in balloons and aeroplanes was, they believed, hindering their careers as they were not gaining experience in the Engineers' more conventional duties and thus missing out on vital promotions. The recruitment net was, therefore, cast wider with officers from other regiments invited to apply. This led to the establishment of the Air Battalion, Royal Engineers – so called because all other ranks came from the Engineers – in February 1911.

Those officers who wished to join the Air Battalion as pilots had to acquire a pilot's licence from the Royal Aero Club or any other recognised European flying organisation (learning to fly in France was popular with well-heeled young officers) and would be refunded £75 upon acceptance into the battalion. They had to be keen; their flying lessons would already have cost them far more than this compensation. Then, as it looked as though war with Germany was imminent, the new First Lord of the Admiralty, Winston Churchill, pushed for non-commissioned officers to be trained as pilots, too. Churchill was a great champion of air power, taking flying lessons himself in 1912 (at the age of 38) until his insurers forbade him. In 1919 he was to become Minister for War and Air. His recommendations about NCO pilots did not work out very well to begin with, not because the NCOs did not make competent pilots, but because they had not enjoyed the same standard of education as the officers, and were unskilled in map reading and poor in making basic calculations. But once these problems were addressed, they began to pass the Air Battalion's pilots' courses in significant numbers. A far more rigorous approach was taken to training than had been in the very early days of the gentlemen aviators, with the Central Flying School opening at Upavon and the first army airfield becoming operational at Netheravon.

By early 1912 the Air Battalion's aeroplane section had moved to a separate camp at Larkhill and it was now abundantly clear that the skills required of the pilots and ground crews were so far removed from the regular activities of the Royal Engineers that the

BELOW: SAMUEL CODY WAS KILLED WHEN HE CRASHED WHILE TESTING HIS LATEST AIRCRAFT DESIGN IN 1913.

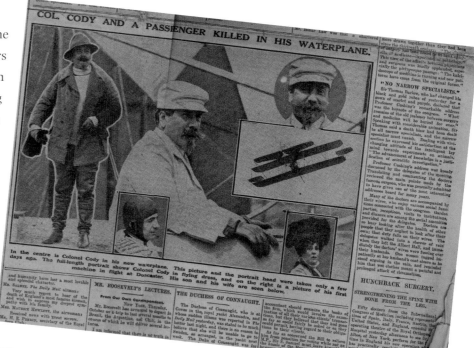

BELOW: SAMUEL CODY WAS KILLED WHEN HE CRASHED WHILE TESTING HIS LATEST AIRCRAFT DESIGN IN 1913.

unit could no longer be considered part of that corps. Consequently the Royal Flying Corps was formed on 13 May. Initially the RFC was a joint service unit with the Army and Navy working together to develop its capabilities, but the Navy soon identified its specific requirements, forming the Royal Naval Air Service. They took responsibility for most of the dirigibles that remained serviceable, the superior range and endurance of the airships being deemed more suitable for maritime reconnaissance, but were also very active in the development of naval aeroplanes. The Army's Royal Flying Corps was left to build itself up to a nominal strength of 131 aircraft in seven different squadrons. Naturally, they also continued their work with tethered balloons, which had now developed into 'kite balloons' of the familiar barrage balloon shape, their horizontal 'tail' surfaces and streamlined shape giving them better stability in adverse wind conditions.

By the time the war with Germany did finally erupt in 1914, the RFC was equipped with a number of different aircraft types. They flew Blériot and Henri Farman monoplanes, the Avro 504, RE 5 and BE 2 biplanes, all destined to become reconnaissance and light bombers when squadrons 2, 3, 4 and 5 finally arrived at

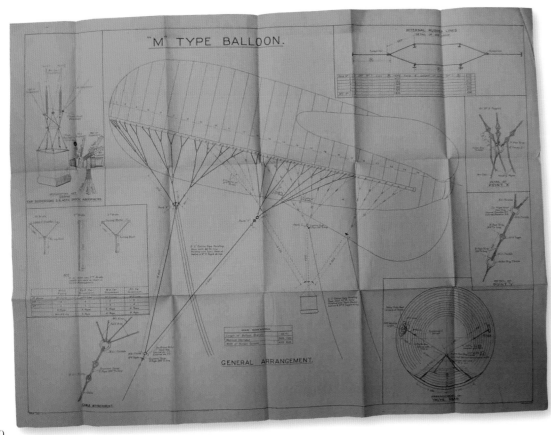

"M" TYPE BALLOON.

GENERAL ARRANGEMENT.

LEFT: ORIGINAL PLANS SHOWING PART OF THE RIGGING ON AN 'M TYPE' KITE BALLOON.

BELOW: A TYPICAL KITE BALLOON TAKES TO THE AIR UNDER THE WATCHFUL EYES OF ITS GROUND CREW.

Maubeuge in August 1914 ready to commence operations. They totalled 45 aeroplanes, 105 officers and 755 other ranks. Back home, 1 Squadron had been held in reserve and to defend Britain against the expected Zeppelin attacks while 6 and 7 Squadrons were assigned a training role.

A year later, just before the Battle of Loos, the RFC strength in France had increased to 12 squadrons and over 160 aircraft. By the time of the first Battle of the Somme in July 1916, there were 27 squadrons with over 420 operational aircraft and over 200 aeroplanes under repair or in reserve. The quality and reliability of the aeroplanes increased as quickly as their numbers, famous names such as the Nieuport Scout, the Sopwith Camel and Pup, the SE 5 and SPAD tripping off the tongues of schoolboys all over Britain. The aircraft became more specialised – fighter planes being introduced whose sole purpose was to shoot down enemy aircraft – better armed and better equipped. Aircraft like the RE 8 (nicknamed 'Harry Tate' after a popular music hall performer) had a Vickers machine gun mounted to fire forward through the propeller blades, its rate of fire synchronised with the speed of the blades, and twin Lewis guns on a scarf ring around the rear cockpit, turning the observer into an air gunner. Regularly used as an artillery spotter,

the RE 8 could also be equipped with a wireless to send messages in Morse to the batteries below, although carrying the wireless set might mean sacrificing a machine gun as the aircraft struggled to get off the ground when weighed down with both!

At home in Britain, Zeppelin airships launched their first bombing raids against the mainland in January 1915, hitting London in May. They generally flew too high for the RFC aircraft to reach them, but in September 1916, when 16 Zeppelins launched a bombing raid against the capital, a BE 2 flown by Lieutenant Leefe Robinson shot down one of the raiders over Hatfield. He was awarded the Victoria Cross, the first such award ever made for bravery in action in the UK.

The British press, determined to boost morale at home and quickly recognising the fascination held by the general public for the new breed of airborne warriors, turned flying aces like the RFC's Albert Ball and James McCudden into household names. The first RFC Victoria Cross of the war went to 2nd Lieutenant William Rhodes-Moorhouse, the award described in the *London Gazette* on 22 May 1915 as being: 'For most conspicuous bravery on 26th April, 1915, in flying to Courtrai and dropping bombs on the railway line near that station. On starting the return journey he was mortally wounded, but succeeded in flying for 35 miles to his destination, at a very low altitude, and reported the successful accomplishment of his object. He has since died of his wounds.'

As always, the aviators were heavily outnumbered by their support staff and ground crews but the pilots and observers were not the only RFC personnel the ground crews were putting in the air during the war. The RFC remained responsible for the observation balloons that continued to be used for artillery spotting throughout the war. The balloons were so important that they were priority targets for fighter pilots of both sides. Belgian ace Willy Coppens shot down 34 German balloons during the course of the war. The balloons were also favourite targets for enemy artillery. The gunners knew that even if they didn't score a direct hit, the shrapnel from a near-miss air burst was likely to wound or kill those in the balloon's basket and stood a very good chance of puncturing the envelope. One man who knew exactly what it was like to be whisked aloft in the basket of a kite balloon in full view of the enemy was Flight Sergeant W. S. Lewis, who wrote about his

experiences in *Everyman At War* in 1930. Lewis described how he and an officer ascended to 5,000 feet at dawn to try to spot an enemy artillery piece that had been laying down harassing fire on the Allied lines at Vimy Ridge. '. . . the enemy developed an astonishing accuracy in shelling kite balloons with shrapnel. I had some uncomfortable half hours with this kind of attack. This morning in May one shell burst towards our balloon, only one, but it left us guessing as to when the next would be sent over.'

But shrapnel from that one shell must have damaged the balloon envelope and it tore itself apart a few moments later. Lewis and his officer extricated themselves from the mess of balloon fabric just in time to jump. They were supplied with parachutes, but the harness fastened only around the thighs and waist and Lewis felt his parachute pack slipping off before he pulled the toggle to release his chute. The cords became tangled round his

BELOW: THE GROUND CREW HANDLING THIS FARMAN AIRCRAFT SHOW THAT THE EARLY RFC WAS A JOINT SERVICE ARMY/NAVY OPERATION.

1878 – 1918

neck and as the parachute started to open, he was slowly being strangled as he fell through the air. He recalled that: 'The sensation was horrible . . . my face seemed to swell to twice its size and my eyeballs seemed too big for their sockets.'

By some miracle, he managed to struggle free, his neck torn and bruised by the cords, but he drifted earthwards for only a few more moments before he came to an abrupt, shuddering halt. The parachute had wrapped itself around the balloon's winch cable. As he dangled there, Lewis could see the billowing canopy of his officer's parachute way below him. Then the parachute began to slip, worked its way loose and he was plummeting earthwards again, the torn parachute flapping uselessly above him. Thoughts of a moment's excruciating pain of shattering bones as he hit the ground flashed through his mind before he felt a bizarrely soft impact. He had landed on top of his officer's parachute, collapsing it. He apologised as both men continued to fall before the parachute suddenly opened again. Miraculously both men landed safely, with Lewis clinging to part of the officer's harness.

In August 1917, recommendations were made to the War Ministry about the future of aerial warfare by Lieutenant General

ABOVE: THE RFC SERVED IN EVERY THEATRE DURING THE FIRST WORLD WAR. THIS BE2 CRASHED IN PALESTINE.

RIGHT: A WAAC DRIVER SERVING WITH THE ROYAL FLYING CORPS IN 1917. RIGHT INSET: ROYAL FLYING CORPS GROUND CREW WITH THEIR AIRFIELD AMBULANCE.

Jan Smuts. His report concluded that: 'there is absolutely no limit to the scale of its future independent war use. And the day may not be far off when aerial operations with their devastation of enemy lands and destruction of industrial and populous centres on a vast scale may become the principal operations of war.'

Smuts advised that a new air service should be formed that would be treated on a par with the Royal Navy and the Army. On 1 April 1918, the RFC became the Royal Air Force. It was the world's first, and the world's largest, independent air force. The new service adopted the Army's assets, equipment and personnel on the understanding that it would continue to provide all necessary support to the Army but, for the time being at least, the Army had lost its Air Corps.

'. . . MY FACE SEEMED TO SWELL TO TWICE ITS SIZE AND MY EYEBALLS SEEMED TOO BIG FOR THEIR SOCKETS.'

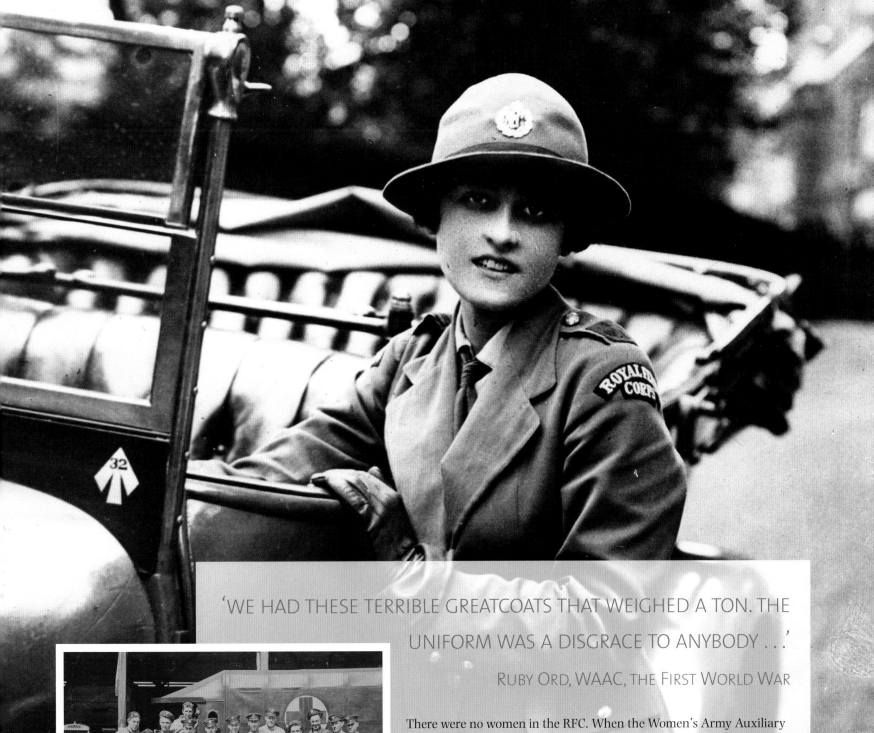

'WE HAD THESE TERRIBLE GREATCOATS THAT WEIGHED A TON. THE
UNIFORM WAS A DISGRACE TO ANYBODY …'

RUBY ORD, WAAC, THE FIRST WORLD WAR

There were no women in the RFC. When the Women's Army Auxiliary
Corps was formed in 1917, women served with many branches of the
Army as cooks, clerks, waitresses, driver-mechanics and as ambulance
crews. There were 57,000 WAACS and more than 10,000 worked at
RFC bases at home and abroad, although RFC ground crews continued
to man their own airfield ambulances (see left).

WAACs like Ruby Ord were poorly paid and held no official service
ranks – they 'enrolled' as WAACs rather than enlisting – yet the majority serving at RFC bases
chose to transfer to the WRAF when it was formed in 1918.

CHAPTER TWO

AIRBORNE OBSERVERS AND
INVADERS 1918 – 1945

At the end of the First World War, the RAF was the world's largest air force with around 20,000 aircraft fulfilling a variety of roles from heavy bomber and transport aeroplanes to ground attack and fighter aircraft. The Army had lost its Air Corps to the new RAF service but was assured of close cooperation, especially since many of the most senior RAF officers maintained strong contacts within their old Army units. Unfortunately, circumstances unfolded that were to erode the relationship between the Army and the RAF.

In the aftermath of the war, the government savagely slashed its military budget, tightening their nation's' economic belt following the huge expenditure of the war years. In less than fifteen years, the RAF was reduced to a force of fewer than 1,000 aircraft. Many of the senior officers whose personal contacts with the Army had promised to smooth the path of inter-service cooperation had retired and both services had, in any case, concentrated their efforts and resources on developing the capabilities required for modern warfare – the type of warfare that had evolved during the battles of 1914–18. The Army was preoccupied with building a mechanised fighting force (including new, much improved, tanks) which promised to make future conflicts far more fluid than the static trench warfare of the first World War.

The RAF, on the other hand, was far more concerned in finding ways to fulfil its new role. The Minister for War and Air, Winston Churchill, stated in Parliament in December 1919 that, 'The first duty of the RAF is to garrison the British Empire.' As well as defending the UK and developing a strategic bomber force, the RAF was to take on the role of 'Air Policing', exerting control over vast territories with a minimum of expenditure. When the activities of Mohammed bin Abdullah (known as 'The Mad Mullah') began to cause serious problems in British

Somaliland on the Horn of Africa, the RAF dealt with the situation in an efficient and cost-effective manner by bombing bin Abdullah's supporters out of their strongholds and harassing them on the ground. They would go on to mount further policing, or 'Air Control' actions in Iraq, India's North-West Frontier and Afghanistan, working with local forces or British Army units, but also deploying their own troops in armoured cars, the precursors of the RAF Regiment. While both the Army and the Navy had been clamouring for the disbandment of the RAF after the First World War and the return of their own air assets, the RAF now looked as though it was showing the older services how to get the job done.

What this meant for the Army was that the original reason for putting men into the air was now being seriously neglected. Observation, especially for artillery spotting, was not being developed in a way that would allow it to keep pace with the speed at which the situation could change on a modern battlefield. The problem was not being overlooked entirely. In 1933 Captain H. J. Parham of the Royal Artillery wrote an article in the *Journal of the Royal United*

LEFT: SECRETARY OF THE ROYAL ARTILLERY FLYING CLUB CAPTAIN CHARLES BAZELEY WAS TASKED WITH EVALUATING AIRCRAFT FOR ARTILLERY OBSERVATION.

Services Institute criticising the existing system of calling in an RAF Army Cooperation aircraft from a distant airfield where the pilot would be briefed on a situation that would doubtless have changed by the time he had arrived in the area of operations. What was needed, Parham argued, was a light aircraft that could operate from a makeshift airstrip alongside the gun batteries and would be flown by a qualified gunnery officer who could direct fire using two-way radio.

In a further essay Parham wrote: 'If we are to do any part of our own observation, the observer and pilot must be one and the same person as only the pilot can ensure that the aircraft is in a suitable position at the crucial moment. It may well be asked "What is the difference between teaching an airman to be a gunner and a gunner to be an airman?"

'The answer is, of course, "It is not intended, nor is it necessary, that the gunner's flying training should be so comprehensive as that of an RAF pilot." All that is required of the gunner pilot is that he should be able to fly a light unarmed aeroplane sufficiently well to enable him to carry out observation at the same time.'

Parham found ready support for his ideas within the ranks of the Royal Artillery Flying Club which formed at Larkhill in 1934. Using private light aircraft, the club secretary, Captain Charles Bazeley, conducted unofficial trials and in 1935 was seconded to the RAF as an Army Cooperation pilot. This only served to convince him that the current system for air observation was hopelessly inadequate. When the RAF re-equipped its Army Cooperation squadrons with the new Lysander aircraft in 1938, Bazeley remained unconvinced of the merits of the new aeroplane. It could certainly take off from an impressively short strip and had a high wing that allowed for good ground visibility but it was also large and cumbersome. Bazeley did not think that it would fare well against enemy fighter aircraft.

With the support of his superior officer, Brigadier H. R. S. Massey (President of the RA Flying Club), Bazeley campaigned for a smaller, lighter observation aircraft and he was ultimately given the go-ahead in December 1938 to conduct trials for a Flying Observation Post at Larkhill. They experimented with different tactics and in evading mock attacks from Spitfires, flying a variety of aircraft that included the American Taylorcraft and Stinson Voyager. Rather than cruising into the observation area at

ABOVE: CAPTAIN H. J. PARHAM OF THE ROYAL ARTILLERY CAMPAIGNED VIGOROUSLY FOR INDEPENDENT ARMY AIRBORNE OBSERVERS.

altitude, they hurtled in a tree-top height then shot into the air to observe the fall of the artillery shells before dropping down to the deck again. This way they avoided exposing themselves to 'enemy' fire and, by never popping up in the same place twice, they could keep the opposition guessing. The trials were still under way in September 1939 when Hitler invaded Poland.

Bazeley was given permission to continue his trials in France during joint exercises with the French, who were experimenting with the autogiro for air observation. He took three Taylorcraft, modified by a manufacturer in Leicester who produced the aircraft under licence, and a Stinson Voyager to France in April 1940 as D Flight, Royal Air Force, Air Observation Post, but had barely commenced range trials with British and French artillery when the Germans began their unstoppable surge westwards. Bazeley was ordered to return home and to disband his unit on arrival, but

'... WE HAVEN'T COME THIS FAR TO GIVE UP NOW'

told the personnel accompanying him, 'We haven't come this far to give up now.' Instead of returning to Old Sarum as instructed, Bazeley took his Air Observation Post to the School of Artillery at Larkhill, hiding out there until the Army could have the disbandment order countermanded.

Following the Allied withdrawal from Dunkirk, Bazeley, by now Major, pushed D Flight forward to participate in every possible training exercise, earning praise from one corps commander who stated that his officers were '... unanimous that the Air OP proved its value to the hilt. As a result of this exercise, I find it difficult to see why the Air OP should remain a part of the RAF.'

Nevertheless, the AOP did remain part of the RAF. The Royal Artillery provided the pilots and army support crews while the aircraft mechanics, administrators and the aeroplanes came from the RAF, the first AOP squadron being formed in August 1941 as 651 Squadron. It was to be followed by two further squadrons, pilots being chosen on the grounds that an AOP flyer had to be a proven gunnery officer first and foremost. The Army had taken a

giant leap towards getting its soldiers back into the air.

In April 1942 Major Bazeley's 651 Squadron was equipped with the latest version of the Taylorcraft, the British Taylorcraft Auster AOP Mk 1, to be known forever more as the Auster. The Auster (the name means 'south wind') was to prove itself in battle along with the men of the AOP when Bazeley took 651 Squadron to North Africa in late 1942. They were involved in their first action in Tunisia on 25 November and from then onwards became indispensable not only as artillery spotters but also for tactical reconnaissance. The temptation for senior officers to make use of them as convenient 'air taxis' had to be strongly resisted.

The AOP expanded continuously throughout the war to a strength of sixteen squadrons which served in North Africa and Italy, where a handful of pilots from 655 Squadron flew over 240 sorties in 30 days, directing 108 artillery shoots in support of the

BELOW: D FLIGHT'S STINSON VOYAGER IS MANHANDLED BY THE GROUND CREW IN FRANCE IN 1940.

28

1918 – 1945

ABOVE: ALTHOUGH AN AMERICAN DESIGN, THE AUSTER WAS MANUFACTURED UNDER LICENCE IN THE UK AND DEVELOPED SPECIFICALLY FOR ITS ROLE WITH THE AOP, SERVING IN EVERY THEATRE FROM NORTHERN EUROPE AND NORTH AFRICA TO THE FAR EAST DURING THE SECOND WORLD WAR.

Anzio landings. Seven AOP Squadrons were involved in Operation Overlord's D-Day landings, with an advance party from 662 Squadron arriving on the Normandy beachhead just an hour after the first assault troops, fighting their way inland to establish a landing strip. AOP aircraft were soon in action in France with an Auster directing the fire from HMS *Rodney*'s huge 16-inch guns during the bombardment of Caen.

656 Squadron operated in Burma from early 1944, where, in common with all AOP units, they fought shoulder to shoulder with the troops on the front line. On one besieged hilltop position, Reg Bailey of C Flight found himself manning a trench alongside a friend, both holding grenades in their hands as they peered out into the darkness where they knew that Japanese troops were massing. 'We also had a couple of loaded Sten guns in front of our trenches. The plan as far a Tubby Charrington and I were concerned . . . was that we would hurl all our grenades, then

empty the Sten into them, and then take to our rifles and bayonets. As a last resort we had a machete laying at our sides. One thing was certain that we, like the rest of the people on that hill, never intended to be taken prisoner.'

During the course of the war, over sixty AOP pilots were lost on active service, with at least nine falling to accidental hits from friendly shells. Among the many decorations awarded to AOP personnel there were more than a hundred DFCs, ten MBEs and two DSOs.

While Bazeley's AOP kept Army interests aloft in the Auster, a new form of Army flying was about to evolve. Inspired by the Germans' success with the use of parachute and glider troops during their campaign in the Low Countries, on 22 June 1940 Winston Churchill demanded of the War Office that they create an airborne force of around 5,000 men. With the Allies having been defeated on mainland Europe and a desperate defence of the homeland

ABOVE: WITH NO ARRESTER HOOK FITTED, THE CREW OF THE ESCORT CARRIER HMS *KHEDIVE* HAD TO RESTRAIN THIS 656 SQUADRON AUSTER WHEN IT LANDED ON DECK DURING THE INVASION OF RANGOON IN MAY 1945.

beginning to rage overhead in the Battle of Britain, the RAF was under extreme pressure. Quite where they were to find the crews and aircraft to train such a huge parachute force, they had no idea.

Nevertheless, the creation of an airborne division forged ahead, although one official report in August 1940 questioned the viability of operational parachute drops when it stated that, 'We are beginning to incline to the view that dropping troops from the air by parachute is a clumsy and obsolescent method and that there are far more important possibilities in gliders.' The great advantage of a

glider was that it could deliver troops and equipment to the battlefield, together, without the delays involved in rallying paratroops scattered over a wide area. It was decided that gliders should form a major part of Churchill's new airborne force.

To overcome the shortage of aircrew, volunteer glider pilots were recruited not only from the RAF but from all ranks of the Army, prompting one Air Staff missive in December 1940 questioning the wisdom of the recruitment policy. 'The idea that semi-skilled, unpicked personnel (infantry corporals have, I

ABOVE: THIS LOCALLY-MADE RECOVERY TRAILER, TOWED BY A DODGE 13CWT TRUCK, SAW SERVICE WITH 656 SQUADRON IN BURMAH IN 1944.

believe, even been suggested) could with a maximum of training be entrusted with the piloting of these troop carriers is fantastic. Their operation is equivalent to forced landing the largest sized aircraft without engine aid – than which there is no higher test of piloting skill.'

The negative sentiments of that document stand as a tribute to the volunteers who came through the glider pilots' training course. They were given sixty hours' basic flying training in powered aircraft before transferring to the glider training school for twelve weeks tuition on the Hotspur and a further six weeks' advanced

training on the Horsa. The gliders, as well as aircrew and aircraft to act as glider tugs, were initially in short supply, leading to a great deal of frustration among the budding pilots, many of whom requested transfers back to their original units only to be told to have patience. In the meantime, having gone through the stringent RAF Aircrew Selection Board procedure to ensure their suitability as pilots, the trainees also underwent extensive infantry training. Route marches, PT and weapons training turned those who were not already experienced infantrymen into first-class soldiers. A glider pilot, unlike the pilot of a paratroop transport, had to be able

TAYLORCRAFT AUSTER AOP

'IT WAS A BIT LIKE A BICYCLE FRAME
COVERED IN CANVAS . . .'

FORMER AUSTER PILOT

MAJOR NEIL BALDWICK

The first Taylorcraft Auster AOP Mk 1 aircraft entered service with the newly formed 651 Squadron in 1942. They were lightweight aeroplanes with a fabric skin covering a fuselage constructed from tubular steel (the later Mk 9 would have all-metal construction), the large wing giving them a low stalling speed that allowed them to 'loiter', giving the pilot the best possible opportunity to observe the fall of shot from the artillery battery to whom he was relaying instructions.

Originally produced by an American manufacturer, the Taylorcraft was imported and subsequently built under licence by a company based at Thurmaston near Leicester, which carried out a wide range of modifications to make the aircraft suitable for service with the AOP during the Second World War. Although initially considered to be merely a temporary stopgap, the Auster was to prove a versatile and reliable aircraft, serving with the Army for over twenty years.

Easy access to the engine meant that the Auster was a simple machine to service in the field.

SPECIFICATION

→ Engines	Mk 1 – single 90hp Blackburn Cirrus Minor Mk 9 – single 180hp Blackburn Cirrus Bombardier 203
→ Maximum Speed	Mk 9 – 128 mph
→ Rate of climb	Mk 9 – 930 feet/min (282 m/min)
→ Range	Mk 9 – 246 miles
→ Service ceiling	Mk 9 – 18,500 feet (5,600 m)
→ Armament	None
→ Total length	Mk 9 – 23 feet 8 inches (7.5 m)
→ Height	Mk 9 – 8 feet 5 inches (2.5 m)
→ Wing Span	Mk 9 – 36 feet 5 inches (11 m)
→ Maximum weight	Mk 9 – 2130 lb (968 kg)
→ Crew	Maximum 3

to join his passengers on the ground when they went into battle.

The men behind the training regime were Major (later Lieutenant Colonel) John Rock, who was with the regiment from earliest days when the first training facility was established at Ringway, Manchester, and Major George Chatterton. Chatterton was a former RAF fighter pilot who had been injured in an accident and had taken a territorial commission in the Queen's Regiment. He was one of the first volunteers for the new Glider Pilot Regiment and took over as its commanding officer when Rock was sadly killed in a night flying accident. With a wealth of flying experience as well as an infantry background, Chatterton was in the ideal position to ensure that his pilots were not only skilled flyers but also highly trained soldiers.

The pilots practised at first on civilian aircraft from private 'sailplane' flying clubs, but once the new gliders began to arrive, the lion's share of their training was on the Hotspur. The General Aircraft Hotspur first took to the air in November 1940, just seventeen weeks after design work had begun. Over a thousand

Hotspurs were produced and, while they never saw operational service, from the outset they were an integral part of the glider pilot training programme. While the first gliders were built by a specialist company in Yorkshire, Slingsby Sailplanes, many trainees were a little disconcerted to find parts of their plywood-and-canvas aircraft stamped with the names of popular furniture manufacturers. The woodworking skills of the British furniture industry had been pressed into service to help create the glider force. Far from being a flying sideboard, however, the elegant Hotspur handled superbly and prepared the pilots for the next stage of their training at airfields such as Netheravon, Weston on the Green, Stoke Orchard or North Luffenham.

The second glider the pilots encountered was generally the Airspeed Horsa. Like the Hotspur, the Horsa had a two-man crew. It could carry 28 fully-laden troops or over 7000 lb of cargo – enough to

BELOW: THE HOTSPUR GLIDER NEVER SAW ACTIVE SERVICE, BUT IT WAS THE MAINSTAY OF THE GLIDER PILOT TRAINING PROGRAMME.

ABOVE: THE HORSA, FAR LARGER THAN THE HOTSPUR, BECAME THE BRITISH ARMY'S MAIN ASSAULT GLIDER.

accommodate a jeep and a six-pounder anti-tank gun. The Horsa was to become the standard British glider for airborne assault. Huge flaps on its wings allowed it to swoop into the LZ (landing zone) at a heart-stopping dive angle of 70°. Its tricycle undercarriage could be jettisoned to allow a rough-surface landing on skids and the pilot had a full range of flight instruments that allowed him to fly at night or in cloud.

Two other gliders were flown by the Glider Pilot Regiment, the giant General Aircraft Hamilcar which was designed to carry a massive 17,500 lb of cargo or a light tank, and the American Waco, officially known as the Hadrian when in British Army service.

Despite the delays caused by the lack of aircraft, recruitment and training was in full swing by the end of 1941 and an Army Air Corps was formed on 24 February 1942. Initially, the Corps consisted of only the Glider Pilot Regiment but the Parachute Regiment was to join when it was formed in August that year and the Special Air Service Regiment also became part of the Army Air Corps when it was officially formed in April 1944.

The first British glider operation, 'Operation Freshman', was mounted in November 1942 when two Horsas, each carrying fifteen Airborne Engineers, took off from Skitten in the north of Scotland behind their Halifax tugs. They were bound for Norway where they were to link up with local resistance workers to sabotage the Vemork Hydro Electric Plant where heavy water was being produced for Nazi atomic weapons research. A combination of bad weather and engine trouble suffered by one of the Halifax tugs resulted in both Horsas and the stricken Halifax crashing. There were no survivors from the Halifax. The glider survivors, including the wounded, were captured by the Germans, tortured and murdered under Hitler's infamous 'Commando Order'.

The first major glider assault to be mounted came in July 1943 when Allied forces based in North Africa invaded Sicily. Staff Sergeant (later Major) H. N. Andrews, remembers arriving in North Africa at Easter and spending some uncomfortably hot siesta periods 'stripped to our shorts sitting on a groundsheet under a mosquito net tied to an olive tree' during the build-up to the invasion. He was uncertain about the Waco gliders they were to fly as, 'I thought what a pity we hadn't been able to fly our Horsas into action for the first time. Although the Waco was a good plane it didn't carry as many and many of the gliding characteristics were different . . .' Not only were the British Glider Pilots expected to fly the unfamiliar Wacos, they first had to assemble them as the gliders were shipped to North Africa in crates direct from the manufacturers. A number of Horsas were actually flown all the way from the UK to supplement the Waco fleet, with several lost en route, before the invasion was launched on the evening of 9 July.

The Regiment's Commanding Officer, Colonel Chatterton, piloted the first Waco of the 144 gliders to take off on the 450-mile

ABOVE: THE AMERICAN-MANUFACTURED WACO GLIDER WAS RENAMED THE HADRIAN FOR SERVICE WITH THE BRITISH ARMY.

RIGHT: MAJOR GEORGE CHATTERTON OVERSAW A RIGOROUS TRAINING REGIME THAT TURNED HIS GLIDER PILOTS INTO HIGHLY SKILLED SOLDIERS. GLIDER PILOTS HAD TO FIGHT ALONGSIDE THEIR PASSENGERS AFTER THE LANDING.

flight across the Mediterranean. He was also one of the first to fall short of his target. Strong winds, navigational errors and the inexperience of some of the tug pilots meant that almost seventy of the gliders were released too early and failed to make the coast. Chatterton and his passengers were able to swim ashore, others were picked up by ships of the amphibious landing force, but more than 300 airborne troops drowned. Less than half of the 2,000-strong glider force arrived in Sicily, yet they still achieved their objectives, against fierce opposition, to help smooth the way for the amphibious assault the following morning. A further glider operation four nights later saw ten Horsas and seven Wacos flying a section of the 1st Parachute Brigade's Royal Artillery Anti-Tank Battery into action to support a parachute force in the capture the Primasole Bridge. Eleven of the gliders were shot down along with many of the Dakotas carrying the paratroops, but the bridge was captured. The Sicilian adventure proved that, although a high casualty rate had to be expected, air landing troops and equipment

by glider was an effective means of delivering an invasion force.

When the long-awaited invasion of Northern Europe was launched on 6 June 1944, gliders formed an essential part of the battle plan. Shortly after midnight six Horsas carrying six platoons of the Ox and Bucks Light Infantry approached their target landing zones. They were to capture and hold two vital bridges over the Caen Canal and River Orne. Flying in darkness, the first of the three gliders assigned to the canal's Bénouville Bridge bridge swooped in towards the eastern bank of the waterway. Piloted by Staff Sergeants

ABOVE: AIRBORNE TROOPS CROSS PEGASUS BRIDGE WITH HORSA GLIDERS ON THEIR LZ IN THE BACKGROUND.

Jim Wallwork and John Ainsworth, as soon as the Horsa's wheels touched the ground, they deployed the arrestor parachute. The glider leapt back into the air, all three wheels torn off, before slamming down on its skids, sending showers of sparks streaming out from beneath the fuselage. An instant later, the nose ploughed into an embankment – the exact spot for which Wallwork and Ainsworth had been aiming. The force of the impact sent both pilots, still strapped in their seats, flying out through the windscreen. Along with their passengers, they were knocked unconscious but would later claim to be the first soldiers of the Allied invasion force to land on French soil – even if they were out cold.

Crew and passengers quickly recovered from their landing

and, with the other two Horsas also landing bang on target, they took the bridge, holding it against fierce opposition until reinforcements arrived. Bénouville Bridge was later renamed Pegasus Bridge in honour of the airborne forces' Pegasus badge. But these were only the first of the glider landings on D-Day. Altogether 220 Horsas and 30 Hamilcars took off for France during the course of the invasion with 212 landing on or near their designated landing zones.

Ken Mead (later Lt Col. Mead) was a glider pilot on D-Day and subsequently at Arnhem. 'What people don't always understand,' he explained, 'is that as soon as a glider cast off it started to drop. You were losing height all the time. You might have only four

'...THERE WERE NO SECOND CHANCES...YOU HAD TO GET IT RIGHT FIRST TIME'

ABOVE: A WAAF OFFICER SKETCHED THESE PORTRAITS OF, FROM LEFT TO RIGHT, CAPTAIN JOHN WALKER, OC 22 FLIGHT; MAJOR JOHN LYNE, OC D SQUADRON; CAPTAIN BARRY MURDOCH, OC 8 FLIGHT; LT S. J. D. MOORWOOD, 8 FLIGHT AND LT IAN MUIR OF 22 FLIGHT.

minutes to identify your landing zone and prepare your approach. There were no second chances. You couldn't go round again. You had to get it right first time.'

The next big glider lift came on 17 September 1944 with the ambitious 'Operation Market Garden' plan to secure a swift route into Germany by capturing bridges over the River Waal at Nijmegen, the River Maas at Grave and the River Rhine at Arnhem.

The British airborne forces at Arnhem found themselves on landing zones too far from the bridge and the strength of the opposition standing against them turned the Arnhem operation into a heroic failure. The glider contingent consisted of 698 aircraft, more than eighty-five per cent of which landed successfully. More than sixty gliders were shot down or lost through accidents and thirteen landed outside the target area.

Sergeant R. G. Wilson was Second Pilot in a Horsa carrying a five-man field gun crew, their gun, limber and jeep. After casting off from the Dakota tug, the Horsa made its approach to the LZ and began its landing dive. Wilson later recalled that, 'When we were about two hundred feet from the ground the glider began to shudder and rock and we realised that we were being fired at. I turned to see why Jock [the First Pilot] was not pushing hard down on the control column at his side and saw him slumped on his side.' With his first pilot dead, Wilson landed the glider on his own and

joined the gun crew as they disembarked before fighting for the next nine days as an infantryman.

Lieutenant Mike Dauncey was among the other 1,000 glider pilots who joined the battle at Arnhem. Dauncey led several attacks and counter-attacks in defence of the artillery positions to which he was assigned, capturing several German prisoners, a machine gun and a number of Luger pistols in the process. He was later wounded by shrapnel in the eye but fought on only to be shot in the leg the following day before having his jaw broken when a grenade landed next to him on his 'blind' side. Dauncey was taken prisoner but escaped from a German prison hospital and was hidden by a Dutch family until he could be smuggled to Allied lines in February 1945. He was returned to the UK and continued to serve with the Army until 1976.

There were many such heroes, but also many who never came home. Sergeant Wilson remembered being evacuated across the Rhine when the 1st Airborne Division was ordered to withdraw and was returned to his airfield at Down Ampney, where he remembers he '. . . went to my billet where the WAAFs had made our beds for those returning. If I remember correctly out of the thirty pilots who occupied that hut only five had returned . . .' The Airborne Division suffered horrendous casualties at Arnhem, with the Glider Pilot contingent losing 157 killed and 469 missing or captured. Major-General Urquhart, commander of the 1st Airborne Division, later wrote a letter of thanks to Colonel Chatterton, stating that, 'Very early in the nine days of the battle it became more and more apparent that we had to call upon the Glider Pilots to the full. They played all kinds of parts, but everything they were asked to do they did whole-heartedly. I am afraid your losses were rather heavy . . .'

March 1945 saw the last major glider operation during the Rhine crossing when 440 British gliders, as well as 906 American Wacos, flew in support of a mass parachute drop on Operation Varsity. Again the gliders proved vulnerable to ground fire, almost all sustaining damage from flak or automatic weapons before reaching their landing zones. Despite this, around ninety per cent of the British force landed on or near their designated LZs. Again the Glider Pilot contingent, including several hundred RAF pilots who had undergone conversion courses to augment the regiment's strength following the Arnhem losses, gave good account of themselves on the battlefield. This was the largest and

RIGHT: GLIDER PILOTS LIKE THESE IN THE RUINS OF A SCHOOL IN
ARNHEM WERE EXPECTED TO JOIN THEIR PASSENGERS TO FIGHT ON THE
GROUND AS INFANTRY.

ABOVE: REGIMENTAL HQ OF THE AIRBORNE LIGHT REGIMENT ON
LANDING ZONE X AT ARNHEM IN THE SHADOW OF THEIR HORSAS'
INTERLOCKED WINGS.

most successful airborne operation in history but, although
elements of the Glider Pilot Regiment had been despatched to
India late in 1944 to prepare for action against the Japanese in
Burma, gliders were never again to be used operationally.

With the end of the Second World War, the Glider Pilot
Regiment was reduced to just one squadron, continuing to train
and demonstrate their unique skills at Netheravon for the next five
years. The Air OP also saw a reduction in their numbers, but theirs
was a role that was now deemed invaluable and the introduction
of the new helicopters towards the end of the war was ultimately
to add a whole new dimension to army flying.

CHAPTER THREE

THE HELICOPTER GOES
TO WAR   1945 – 1957

Just as had happened following the end of the First World War, the end of hostilities in 1945 brought about swingeing cuts in military budgets and manpower. The twelve AOP squadrons that had seen service during the war years were cut to just four. Having fought in North Africa, Sicily and Italy, 651 Squadron was sent to Egypt in 1945. 652 Squadron, which had served in France, Holland and Germany remained in Germany, eventually moving to Detmold in 1949. 657 Squadron returned to England after seeing action in North Africa, Italy, Holland and Germany while the fate of the fourth surviving unit, 656 Squadron, epitomised the problems facing Britain's post-war armed forces.

Although peace had been declared, the fighting was far from over for many of the British service personnel stationed overseas. Military planners were caught between a rock and a hard place in the post-war years, facilitating the expected massive reductions in operational strength, yet facing unexpected and increasing demands for commitments worldwide. 656 Squadron should have seen their operational duties scaled down dramatically following the Japanese surrender but, having served in India and Burma since 1943, in 1945 the squadron became engaged in the turmoil that evolved in the Dutch East Indies as the Dutch struggled to reclaim their territory following an uprising by Indonesian nationalists. B Flight was despatched to Semarang from where they flew artillery spotting and reconnaissance missions, even, on occasion, in support of Japanese troops who were fighting alongside the Dutch and British.

The conflict was to have a direct influence on future events in Malaya and Borneo, the peace deal that was finally brokered in 1949 leading to an independent Indonesia. For 656 Squadron, the end of the fighting meant being withdrawn to Singapore where it was reduced to just a single flight. Little

over a year later, in 1948, the squadron was restored to full strength when the Malayan Emergency erupted.

The squadron was initially reformed at Sembawang Royal Naval Air Station in Singapore with elements of its four flights operating from various bases across the peninsula including Seramban, south of Kuala Lumpur; Tai Ping further north on the west coast and isolated forward airstrips such as the one at Benta. Benta was a typical rough landing strip hacked out of the jungle by the Japanese during the Second World War. By 1950, Squadron Headquarters had been established at Noble Field in Kuala Lumpur, but elements of the flights were 'rotated' through the forward operating bases and places like Benta became home to each of them for weeks at a time. The accommodations enjoyed by the squadron during the war years had included two fine houses with sea views on the coast in the north of the country at Kuala Trengganu, where the Austers' runway was a beautiful grass strip on the local golf course. There the squadron had been incredibly popular

LEFT: THE *PEGASUS DAILY* KEPT EVERYONE IN JAVA UP TO DATE WITH NEWS FROM HOME AND THE FAR EAST.

ABOVE: B FLIGHT'S VICTORIOUS FOOTBALL TEAM IN SEMARANG, JAVA IN 1946.

RIGHT: IN HONG KONG, THERE WAS A FULL PROGRAMME OF FESTIVITIES FOR 1903 FLIGHT IN 1949.

43

with the locals, organising football matches and being taught 'ronging', Malayan dancing. The Scottish contingent soon realised that Malayan music was also suited to Scottish country dancing and reciprocated by teaching the locals a few reels.

Airfields like Benta were a complete contrast, with only a few thatched huts and tents to provide shelter from the searing sun or monsoon storms and the aircraft standing out in the open. Dense morning mists often prevented any flying before around 9a.m. and by late afternoon fierce electrical storms could leave the aircraft grounded. Nevertheless, most of the pilots found themselves flying 90 hours or more every month. In 1955, the squadron's thirty-four aircraft clocked up 22,000 hours on operations and by 1960 they had amassed a total of more than 150,000 hours.

Pete Biggadike remembers being posted to Kluang in 1957.

'At that time there were three RAF airmen, one Army driver, a pilot and one Auster aircraft based there. My first stay at Kluang lasted for about six weeks and during that time we were all on duty twenty-four hours a day. We were responsible for all visiting aircraft as well as operating our own Auster AOP Mk9. There was virtually no off-duty time and visits to Kluang town were mainly for military reasons. Curfews were in operation and many areas were out of bounds because of terrorist activities in the locality. Being isolated on the airfield it was prudent to have a weapon available, particularly at night time. This was usually a .303 rifle

44

1945 – 1957

ABOVE: AN OFF-DUTY MOMENT AT TAI PING IN 1955

RIGHT: THERE'S NO PLACE LIKE HOME, AND SEREMBAN WAS CERTAINLY
NO PLACE LIKE MIDDLE WALLOP.

with fifty rounds of ammunition which was normally carried in
the Auster during a sortie.

'As the security situation improved I managed to visit Kluang
town, sometimes having the occasional glass of Tiger or a bottle of
Anchor beer at the Paramount Hotel. However, any entertainment
for us was very limited. There was no television and listening to the
radio or reading were the main activities in our tin hut
accommodation. Sometimes we would chat on the telephone with
the operators at the telephone exchange to relieve the boredom.'

Most of the flying in Malaya was reconnaissance work, there
being little opportunity for artillery shoots against the enemy
Communist Terrorists (CTs) in the jungle. Instead, the pilots scoured
the jungle areas searching for CT camps, where the guerrillas would

ABOVE: A THATCHED WORKSHOP IN TAI PING

often clear areas of the jungle to cultivate crops. These would be carefully plotted on a map and then either an air strike would be called in to obliterate the camp or troops would be sent in on the ground. Navigation in the jungle is notoriously difficult, so foot patrols would make smoke or send up a balloon to show their position and an Auster flying above would then radio course corrections to guide them towards the target CT camp. Austers used to mark targets for bomber formations were equipped with bomb racks to drop parachute flares over the target. Ken Mead, who converted to Austers when the GPR's gliders were phased out in 1950, flew several target marking sorties. He remembers these having to be executed with immaculate timing. 'The bomber

formation leader would count down to "bombs away" from about ten minutes out,' he recalled. 'Our job was to drop flares over the target. We did that with just forty seconds to go. The bombers were flying at 8,000 feet, but we dropped our flares from treetop height. Then you got out of there as quick as you could.' When the Lincoln bombers each delivered their fourteen 1000 lb bombs, the Auster pilots were still close enough to feel the blast wave rock their aircraft.

Although the target marker Austers used VHF radios to communicate with the bomber flights, prior to 1955 very few were so equipped, pilots using a standard Army HF set which involved deploying a hundred feet of trailing aerial once airborne. Pilots who neglected to crank the aerial back onto its reel before landing were for the high jump.

As well as reconnaissance and target marking, the Austers in

'. . . WE DROPPED OUR FLARES FROM TREETOP HEIGHT. THEN GOT OUF THERE AS QUICKLY AS WE COULD . . .'

1945 – 1957

ABOVE LEFT: FITTING A FLARE TO A 656 SQUADRON AUSTER.

ABOVE RIGHT: AN AUSTER OVERFLIES A COLUMN OF MARKER SMOKE IN MALAYA.

RIGHT: A BOX OF NO 80 GRENADES WEIGHING AROUND 140 LB WAS ABOUT THE HEAVIEST LOAD THAT COULD BE DROPPED INTO THE JUNGLE FROM AN AUSTER.

Malaya were tasked with dropping propaganda leaflets to the CTs and even, despite their limited payload, dropping supplies to patrols operating in the jungle. They were also used as 'Light Liaison' flights, as VIP transport, and they were involved in searching for downed aircraft, several Austers amongst them. Pilots caught out by the sudden onset of a tropical storm could easily find themselves in difficulties. Once an aircraft was swallowed up by the jungle canopy, it became incredibly difficult to spot from the air. An essential part of jungle flying, therefore, was survival training. Many pilots survived harrowing experiences in the jungle but the example that is still cited at the Jungle Warfare School is that of Sergeant K. G. McConnell who emerged from the hills over three weeks after his aircraft crashed. He had help from jungle tribespeople along the way but had made his epic trek on a

painfully broken ankle. Sadly, seven pilots were lost in jungle crashes, among them Captain Churcher of 1907 Flight who was flying Brigadier Erskine from Mentakas to Kuala Lumpur. Their aircraft was not discovered for five years and no sign of their bodies was ever found.

But it wasn't only the weather and the jungle that made Malayan flying a hazardous business. In 1955 Captain Masters of 1914 Flight was commencing his descent into Noble Field when he saw a huge

ABOVE: The survival handbook issued to pilots. Their lives could depend on their survival skills if they crashed in the jungle.

LEFT: An RAF Sycamore struggles into the air carrying the remains of a crashed Auster.

BOTTOM: Major L. J. Wheeler of 656 Squadron inspects an RAF Dragonfly in Malaya.

ABOVE: AN AUSTER 6 OF 1903 FLIGHT AT FORT GEORGE IN KOREA, 1952.

snake slither up from behind the instrument panel, climbing one of the forward canopy supports. When he received no response to his urgent request for a straight-in approach, he did so anyway, with the snake now making its way rearwards above his head. He switched off as he touched down and it was said that the aircraft was still on the move when he dismounted. The snake disappeared through an inspection panel and the ground crew had to remove the whole wing before they could capture the four-and-a-half-foot monster.

The Malayan Emergency was to drag on for twelve long years but it was not the only place where the Army flyers saw active service in the years following the Second World War. In the Middle East, 651 Squadron were heavily involved in operations in Palestine up to 1955 but also made its presence felt in Eritrea, where newly qualified pilot John (later Major John) Dicksee spent two years from 1951. 'We were trying to help keep the peace between warring factions while the UN decided whether to give the place independence or make it part of Ethiopia,' he recalled.

'We were basically helping the civil police who were falling apart. The best thing about it was that we had a lot of independence. Our Commander, Royal Artillery, who was responsible for the military side of things, lived in the canal zone and never came to see us. And the Air Officer Commander, who held sway over our flying activities, lived in Aden, so only occasionally visited. Most people didn't know where Eritrea was and there was no world wide communication in those days which meant that Whitehall wasn't interfering.

'I flew an Auster Mk6 and I only bent one! I was flying early on a Sunday morning in support of an infantry platoon and they had written a message in the sand below. I looked out over the side to try and read it and failed to pay proper attention to what I was doing and I stalled the engine and crash-landed in a field of corn. The plane was a write-off but I got out unscathed because you crashed fairly slowly in those days!'

In May 1950, the Army Air Corps that had been formed in 1942 was formally disbanded. Many of the pilots then still with the Glider Pilot Regiment were retrained on the Auster and when 1913 Light Liaison Flight joined 1903 AOP Flight in Korea, its officers, warrant officers and sergeants continued to wear their GPR regimental insignia. The winter weather in Korea presented problems that were a far cry from tropical torment of Malaya or

ABOVE: THE CARAVAN AND TENTS THAT FORMED PART OF THE
OPERATIONAL HQ AT FORT GEORGE.

RIGHT: SAC SHAW AND LAC DOWNES EXAMINE A STRIP OF RECON
PHOTOS OUTSIDE 'THE CARAVAN' AT FORT GEORGE.

the more temperate and temperamental weather at Middle Wallop.
Major-General P. A. Downward was a Captain and commander of
1913 Flight in Korea. He later wrote in the *Journal of the British
Korean Veterans Association* that he had arrived in Korea in the
autumn of 1951 'with six pilots, all belonging to the Glider Pilot
Regiment and five aircraft, all brand new Auster Mk 6s. These we
had put together at Iwakuni in Japan and flown across the sea and
up the Korean peninsula until we finally reached the Fort George
airstrip alongside the Imjin River.

'The strip had only just been completed and the surface was
very soft and extremely muddy. As each of us landed, it was as
though we had landed on a carrier deck as we came to a sudden
standstill within ten yards of touchdown . . . very different to the
rolling touchdowns we had been used to in the fields around
Middle Wallop . . .'

1945 – 1957

Neither were they to find their billets as comfortable as those they had enjoyed at Middle Wallop. At Fort George, the unit bedded down in tents or huts known as 'hutchies'. Partly buried in the ground to try to ward off the ferocious cold of the Korean winter, hutchies were heated by the ubiquitous American Army-issue stove that was powered by drip-fed petrol. Inevitably, there were fires, surviving the elements in the field proving once again to be every bit as dangerous as facing up to the enemy.

There was, of course, serious work to be done, with 1903 Flight fulfilling their traditional role by conducting artillery shoots from several thousand feet as well as providing a photo reconnaissance. 1913 Flight shared some of the photography responsibilities, also becoming involved in leaflet drops and ferrying VIPs. While the Austers had no opposition in the air and the Chinese at first paid scant regard to their activities, they soon came to realise the threat posed by the unarmed aircraft. Pilots became adept at dodging small arms and anti-aircraft fire, although the ground crews still regularly found themselves patching up bullet or shrapnel holes. One pilot, Captain Jarvis, found himself in difficulty near the front line and had no choice but to make a forced landing on a rough country road. He coaxed his faltering Auster down, picking out the straightest stretch of road he could find, and was relieved to make a decent landing. If he thought he was safe, however, he really should have checked his Korean Highway Code first. The driver of an oncoming jeep clearly felt that he had right of way and refused to pull off the road, forcing Jarvis to veer off. His must surely be the only Auster to have been damaged in a 'road rage' incident.

ABOVE: LT 'LONG' JOHN SNOW, CAPT 'TINY' IRWIN, SGT JOHN HUTCHINGS, STAFF SGT J. C. ROLLEY, SGT 'RED' MEASTON AND CAPT P. F. WILSON WITH A 1913 FLIGHT AUSTER.

ABOVE LEFT: LEAFLETS LIKE THESE WERE DROPPED BY 1913 FLIGHT OVER CHINESE AND NORTH KOREAN POSITIONS.

BELOW: THE CHIMNEY FROM A US ARMY STOVE PROTRUDES FROM THIS 'HUTCHIE' OCCUPIED BY 1903 FLIGHT GROUND CREW.

ABOVE: THIS AUSTER HAD TO BE DISMANTLED TO BE RETURNED TO FORT GEORGE FOR REPAIRS FOLLOWING A 'ROAD RAGE' INCIDENT!

The most remarkable thing about Korea in terms of Army flying, however, was the widespread use of the helicopter by US forces for troop transport and supply, tactical reconnaissance and casualty evacuation. Their effectiveness did not go unnoticed by the British.

In Europe, meanwhile, where the BAOR units faced the might of the Cold War Warsaw Pact forces across a divided Germany, AOP tactics had been put to the test in exercises in 1950 when Major Peter Mead, the newly appointed commander of 652 Squadron, learned some valuable lessons. 'The "enemy" . . . contained the greater part of the RAF in Germany and they

appeared to have been briefed to eliminate our Air OPs. Had we known this, I doubt if it would have bothered us much; we did not believe the jet fighter pilot could come down close to the ground and "mix it" with us, nor did we believe that he could detect our well-concealed fields and strips.'

Manoeuvres during the exercise involved a strategic withdrawal during which the 'enemy' RAF fighter pilots had a field day.

'As the withdrawal started,' Major Mead recounted, 'so the enemy fighters started to beat us up. One pilot reckoned he had been "shot down" as he took off from his strip, another as he landed. After three days . . . only one of our pilots was left alive.'

'AFTER THREE DAYS . . . ONLY ONE OF OUR PILOTS WAS LEFT ALIVE'

The AOP and light liaison pilots still maintained that, by adapting their tactics and carrying observers, they would be able to evade Soviet fighters which, during a 'live' war, would be flying at speeds far greater than the German fighters they had dodged during the Second World War. Nevertheless, many now began to believe that helicopters, which fly far closer to the ground, ascend and descend rapidly and hide in small forest clearings or even amongst farm buildings would stand a far greater chance of survival.

Helicopters had, in fact, been in limited use with the British armed forces for some time. While early trials with eccentric autogyro machines in the 1930s had proved unsatisfactory, by 1944 an early Sikorsky R4A had seen service in Burma and in 1946 one of 657 Air OP's flights was equipped with Sikorsky R4Bs and later R6B2s for evaluation. These were redesignated as the Hoverfly 1 and 2 in AOP service, Captain P. Wilson conducting the first ever artillery shoot by helicopter on exercise in September 1947, but at the end of the year the helicopter flight was

BELOW: EXTENSIVE TRIALS WERE CONDUCTED WITH THE HOVERFLY AS A POTENTIAL AOP HELICOPTER, ALTHOUGH MAINTENANCE BECAME PROBLEMATIC.

ABOVE LEFT: WHEN THE FIRST JEHU WHIRLWINDS ARRIVED AT MIDDLE WALLOP IN 1956, TRIALS INCLUDED EXPERIMENTS IN 'ROPING DOWN'.

ABOVE RIGHT: DURING TRIALS, ONE OF THE JEHU WHIRLWINDS MADE THE FIRST HELICOPTER LIFT OF 1000 LB IN A CARGO NET.

disbanded. The machines were becoming more and more prone to malfunctions and were proving extremely expensive to keep airworthy. The engines were not easy to work on and a simple plug change – a regular necessity because of oiling up – took hours.

Although the Hoverflies were retired from their AOP duties, better, more efficient machines were on the way. In 1951, 1906 AOP Flight based at Middle Wallop had three Mk II Bristol Sycamore machines which were used for evaluation, liaison and VIP flying, while the RAF was making use of the Sycamore and the Westland Dragonfly in Malaya by 1952. The Dragonfly was an American-designed machine, the Sikorsky S51, built under licence by Westland in Yeovil and fitted with an Alvis Leonides engine. Both the Dragonfly and the Sycamore were plagued by mechanical problems in Malaya, with the Sycamore suffering added indignity when it was discovered that the linseed oil used to protect its laminated wooden rotor blades actually made them rather appetising to the white ant. The Malayan Emergency also saw the Royal Navy deploy their Sikorsky S55 anti-submarine helicopters, stripped of their specialist sonar equipment, to be pressed into service in the jungle while the RAF committed a squadron of Westland Whirlwinds (the S55 manufactured under licence by Westland).

Despite the obvious interest shown by the British armed forces in the new helicopters, it was clear from the Korean experience that the Americans were far ahead of us not only in developing the machines themselves, but also in the tactical use of helicopters. It was decided that a unit should be created to assess the suitability of the helicopter for resupplying Army forward units in the field as well as casualty evacuation and troop transportation. At that time, the most experienced helicopter pilots and ground crews were RAF, leading to the logical conclusion that a large percentage of the unit should be from the air force. In the end, half of the pilots and all of the technical ground crew were drafted in from the RAF while the rest of the pilots were officers from the Royal Artillery and RASC. The RASC also provided the new unit's non-technical personnel.

On 1 April 1955, the Joint Experimental Helicopter Unit (JEHU) was formed at Middle Wallop under the command of Lieutenant-Colonel J. F. T. Scott with Squadron Leader D. C. L. Kearns as his number two. Initially they had just six Mk 14 Sycamores and it would be a full year before they received a further six Mk 2 Whirlwinds. Initial trials involved evaluating the machines' troop carrying and load lifting capabilities. Ground

SKEETER AOP 12

'IT WAS LIKE A KID'S TOY WITH A FAN ON TOP ...'

LT COL. (RETD) DEREK ARMITAGE

The Skeeter officially entered service with the Army Air Corps in 1958 but had been previously been under development for over ten years first by Cierva and later by Saunders-Roe. The first model was fitted with wooden rotor blades that were cured in a local baker's oven near the Cierva company's Eastleigh plant. While the original prototype showed promise, it was clearly underpowered and the 106 hp Jameson engine was gradually upgraded until the final AOP 12 model received a 215 hp de Havilland Gypsy unit. Orders were placed for 64 Skeeter AOP 12s.

There remained, however, problems with the power delivery and, while the Skeeter was eventually cleared to operate in extreme cold having been tested in temperatures as low as -35° C in Canada in 1959, it failed to achieve the required rate of vertical climb in hot and humid conditions when it was tested in Aden the same year at +35° C. Most pilots agreed, however, that the Skeeter was easy to fly and highly manoeuvrable. The aircraft's sphere of operations was restricted to northern Europe where it served in a reconnaissance and AOP role with the BAOR.

SPECIFICATION

→ Engines	1 x de Havilland Gypsy Major 4 cylinder, in-line, fuel injected 6.9 litre producing 215 hp
→ Cruise Speed	90 mph
→ Never Exceed Speed	121 mph
→ Service ceiling	12,800 ft (3,900 m)
→ Range	213 miles (343 km)
→ Armament	None
→ Total length	39 feet (11.88 m)
→ Fuselage Length	26 feet 6 inches (8.07 m)
→ Height	7 feet 6 inches (2.28 m)
→ Main Rotor Span	32 feet (9.75 m)
→ Empty weight	1653 lb (750 kg)
→ Maximum weight	2300 lb (1043 kg)
→ Crew	1 pilot, 1 passenger

ABOVE: A MK 2 WHIRLWIND OF THE JOINT EXPERIMENTAL HELICOPTER UNIT DURING TRIALS IN ENGLAND IN 1956.

crews refined their skills during the exercises and a new specialist qualification of Helicopter Crewman, the predecessor to today's Air Trooper, was introduced. The unit was due to move to BAOR for the Autumn exercises in 1956, but the political situation in Egypt prompted the order for them to make ready for active service overseas. In September JEHU's twelve aircraft and two Army fuel bowsers were aboard the aircraft carrier HMS *Theseus* undergoing carrier flight trials, having previously practised carrier landings on a patch of ground marked out to the dimensions of a flight deck. Little over a month later, they were to go to war.

Egyptian President Colonel Nasser had nationalised the Suez Canal in July 1956, intent on bolstering his failing economy with the operating profits from the Canal. The Canal had been built by the French almost a century before, the Suez Canal Company being jointly owned and run by the British and French. Nasser threatened to imprison any foreign employees of the Suez Canal Company who resigned. With almost two thirds of Europe's oil supplies passing along the waterway, the canal was of vital importance, so Britain and France decided to take it back. Codenamed 'Operation Musketeer', the attack on the Canal involved the Israelis as well as the British and French, and the JEHU aircraft were initially earmarked for casualty evacuation duties.

By the time JEHU's aircraft had embarked on the carrier HMS *Ocean*, the plan had changed and when they rendezvoused with HMS *Theseus* in Malta on 31 October, they practised air lifting troops from 45 Commando. The unit also became the JHU, the 'Experimental' tag being dropped while it was on active service.

Along with the ten Mk 22 Whirlwinds of the Royal Navy's 845 Squadron, they were to undertake the first ever helicopter landings under fire as part of an operational amphibious assault. Both carriers left Malta along with their escorts on 3 November, and two nights later a blackout was imposed. At daybreak on 6 November they were lying nine miles off Port Said, where great palls of smoke from air and sea bombardments already shrouded the shoreline. Once a suitable LZ had been chosen near the de Lesseps statue (the man behind the building of the Canal) at the mouth of the harbour, JHU's aircraft prepared for take-off. Even though they had been stripped of all unnecessary equipment, including doors and the second pilot's seat, the Mk 2 Whirlwind could lift just five fully-equipped marines, the Sycamore only three. On the Sycamores, two of the marines had to sit with their legs outboard, such was the shortage of space. The more powerful Mk 22 Whirlwinds of 845 Squadron, similarly stripped down, could manage seven marines.

With their passengers aboard, the first wave took off at 06.10, the Whirlwinds followed by the Sycamores. They formed up and headed for shore in four 'vics' of three aircraft before being joined by 845 Squadron's Whirlwinds for the final run in. The landings were coordinated in waves with one wave coming in just far enough behind the preceding wave to be able to land as soon as the helicopters in front had disgorged their troops and taken off. This way they achieved the fastest possible build-up of troops on the ground. This all required very precise timing. No one wanted to be standing off at the hover, a sitting duck, while waiting for the LZ to clear. The helicopters and the marines on the ground were, after all, taking heavy incoming fire. The first helicopter to have gone ashore on a solo reconnaissance flight had returned with twenty bullet holes and a wounded pilot.

Despite the enemy fire, the dense smoke and the fact that they

57

1945 – 1957

'. . . SHORTSIGHTED OPPOSITION TO THE UNIT WAS ONCE AGAIN DEFEATED. THERE IS LITTLE DOUBT THAT THIS WAS ENTIRELY DUE TO THE SUCCESS ACHIEVED BY THE JOINT HELICOPTER UNIT AT SUEZ . . .'

ABOVE: WAITING FOR THE ORDER TO START UP ON THE DECK OF HMS *OCEAN*, NINE MILES OFF PORT SAID AT DAWN ON 6 NOVEMBER 1956.

LEFT: ON THE CARRIER FLIGHT DECKS, CHOCKMEN HAD TO LIE BY THE WHEELS HOLDING THE CHOCKS IN POSITION WHEN THE ENGINES WERE STARTED OR WARMING UP.

OPPOSITE: THE JEHU FUEL BOWSERS WERE LOADED ONTO THE AIRCRAFT CARRIERS AND USED TO FUEL THE HELICOPTERS ON DECK WHEN THEY WERE AT SEA.

were running on near-empty tanks to keep their weight down, JHU launched seven waves of aircraft, the last carrying underslung loads. The turnaround time on the deck was less than two minutes, and only four minutes if refuelling was required. In preparation for Musketeer the ground crews (or deck crews in this instance) had worked unstintingly to halve their previous best turnaround times. All of the marines, their weapons and ammunition were ashore by 07.30 and further lifts of stores and equipment continued for another hour until the JHU helicopters and crews had delivered 178 marines and 12 1/2 tons of equipment. Altogether, the combined force of Whirlwinds and Sycamores had between them ferried 415 men and 25 tons of equipment ashore. On their return journeys, they fulfilled their original role of casualty evacuation, one unfortunate marine having perhaps the quickest turnaround of any wounded soldier. He was hit within minutes of landing, put on the next Whirlwind to leave and was back aboard HMS *Ocean* within twenty minutes of having first left the flight deck. Altogether, the helicopters evacuated ninety-six casualties from the beachhead during the course of the first day.

International political pressure was ultimately to diminish the military success of Operation Musketeer, but the helicopter's great potential had been ably demonstrated. The JHU reverted to being

the JEHU and its aircraft were given a major overhaul, it having been discovered in Egypt that they were suffering badly from salt corrosion. The cost involved in returning the Whirlwinds to Westlands raised a debate about whether the JEHU should remain in existence, but Suez had shown how valuable the helicopter was to become. The official 'Outline History' report on the unit's activities states that, 'Wisdom fortunately prevailed and shortsighted opposition to the unit was once again defeated. There is little doubt that this was entirely due to the success achieved by the Joint Helicopter Unit at Suez, demonstrating indisputably on active service that the load-carrying helicopter could play a vital part in modern mobile warfare.'

The JEHU's trials resumed back at Middle Wallop as soon as their aircraft were serviceable again. The unit participated in

ABOVE: WESTLAND ENGINEER JOHN COOMBS ACCOMPANIED THE JHU TO SUEZ AND IS SEEN HERE INSPECTING A WHIRLWIND AT EL GAMIL AIRFIELD.

training exercises, including practice amphibious landings with the Royal Marines and further training aboard aircraft carriers, but also made history by transmitting the UK's first airborne TV transmissions. The images from the camera equipment installed in a Sycamore were just flickering glimpses of the countryside around Middle Wallop, but the JEHU nonetheless blazed a trail for the widespread use of helicopters in TV filming, something that we all take very much for granted today.

While the JEHU helicopter pilots and ground crews were steadily building an overwhelming case for the helicopter as the

ABOVE: CAPTAIN J. B. SHAW, RASC, ON PATROL OVER PORT SAID IN A
SYCAMORE.

RIGHT: IN 1957, A JEHU SYCAMORE WAS FITTED WITH PLESSEY
BROADCASTING EQUIPMENT TO CONDUCT THE FIRST EVER TELEVISION
TRANSMISSIONS FROM A HELICOPTER.

main element of the Army's future airborne capability, the Auster
crews continued to ply their trade as AOP flights, Light Liaison
Flights and Independent Flights, fulfilling whatever function was
demanded of them. As well as operating at home and with the
BAOR, They were involved in Korea and in Egypt in the Canal Zone
up to 1955. They continued to fly hazardous missions in Malaya
and in Cyprus where the EOKA guerrilla army was battling for

1945 – 1957

ABOVE: ONCE BACK IN BRITAIN, THE JEHU CONTINUED THEIR TRIALS AND THE HELICOPTERS WERE A GREAT CROWD PLEASER WHENEVER THEY WERE CALLED ON TO GIVE DEMONSTRATIONS.

RIGHT: ARMY AND RAF PERSONNEL WORKED TOGETHER ON EXERCISE WITH THE JEHU, ALL GAINING VALUABLE EXPERIENCE OF OPERATING HELICOPTERS IN THE FIELD.

independence from Britain and union with Greece.

There were, however, great changes afoot for the Army's air assets. One of the things helping to push through those changes first arrived at Middle Wallop in January 1956 – the Skeeter. At first glance, the frail machine hardly seemed the sort of aircraft that the supporters of an independent Army air wing could pin their hopes on. The Skeeter had been under development by the Cierva company since 1948. Cierva had designed the autogyro which became the Avro 671 Rota that the RAF's School of Army Cooperation at Old Sarum had experimented with in the mid-thirties. The company also designed the tri-rotor W11 Air Horse

ABOVE: THE SKEETER WAS DESTINED TO BECOME THE FIRST HELICOPTER TO ENTER FULL SERVICE WITH THE ARMY.

which, when it first flew in 1948, was the largest helicopter in the world. Although it was seen as a promising contender for the role of a future Army heavy lift helicopter, the W11 project was abandoned after the first prototype crashed in 1950, killing all three on board. The Skeeter, at the other end of the size scale, was a two-seat light helicopter intended for training and private use. It was to have a price tag of around £3,000 and running costs roughly equivalent to that of a contemporary 20 hp car.

The Mk 1 Skeeter was powered by a 106 hp Jameson engine and early tests showed promise, although it was woefully underpowered. The Mk 2 first flew in 1949 with a 145 hp de Havilland Gypsy Major powerplant but this model displayed disturbing ground resonance problems and eventually destroyed itself on the ground in June 1950. A pair of Mk 3 Skeeters were delivered for evaluation at Boscombe Down in 1951 but , although the handling characteristics were deemed acceptable, the aircraft's performance at altitude or in hot weather was not. The engine was replaced with 180 hp Bristol Bombardier unit and redesignated

the Mk 3b. One of these crashed during testing at the manufacturer's Eastleigh base and the other began to disintegrate while rolling along the ground at just 28 mph. Despite these problems, the Skeeter was seen as the most promising, most cost-effective option to fulfil the Ministry of Supply's requirement for an AOP and reconnaissance helicopter to enter service in 1957.

Saunders Roe had taken control of Cierva in 1951 and continued development of the skeeter, even experimenting with Napier rocket motors on the rotor tips to try to boost the helicopter's performance. This was ultimately deemed impractical and development continued until a Mk 6 Skeeter with a 200 hp Gypsy Major engine was delivered to Middle Wallop for limited trials in January 1956. The two weeks of testing followed by further tests with further updated aircraft ultimately led to an order for sixty-four aircraft, powered by a 215 hp Gypsy Major engine and designated as the Skeeter AOP Mk 12, to be ordered for the Army.

The Skeeter was to become the first helicopter with which the new Army Air Corps was equipped.

CHAPTER FOUR

THE NEW ARMY AIR CORPS
1957 – 1967

I t had become abundantly apparent in the years after the Second World War that the modern Army needed light air support on an ever greater scale. The Army was more mobile than ever before and was expected to be able to react more quickly than ever before. In operational situations that meant that Army commanders required up-to-the minute intelligence and reconnaissance reports, swift resupply of forward units and immediate casualty evacuation.

The RAF could no longer be expected to meet all of the Army's requirements. The financial and logistical burdens of supplying aircraft and technical staff for the AOP and Light Liaison units were responsibilities which, common sense dictated, should better be borne by the Army alone. The idea that the Army should look after its own air assets had, of course, been around even before Bazeley took his experimental AOP flight to France in 1940 but by the mid-fifties re-establishing an Army air cadre made perfect sense. In 1957 it was decided that the Glider Pilot Regiment would finally be disbanded and the AOP and Light Liaison units would merge to form a new Army Air Corps.

This decision, of course, was not made overnight. Discussions had been under way since the end of the Second World War about how much of the RAF's Army Co-operation role should be devolved to the Army and how such a change could be managed. The Army Council had made proposals to the Air Council; the Air Council had put counter-proposals to the Army Council; the Chief of the Imperial General Staff, the War Office and the Air Ministry had exchanged missives with all concerned; the Director of Land/Air Warfare had fired off his own barrage of memos and the confounding issue of the new rotary wing aircraft appeared only to help feed the inertia. The helicopter trials that had been under way since the end

LEFT: CAPTAIN S. PALMER, RA; CAPTAIN R. SMAILES, RA; MAJOR R. MATTHEWS MC, RA; CAPTAIN P. WILKINSON, RA; CAPTAIN M. PAGE, RA AND 'MAIDA', THE 1908 INDEPENDENT AOP FLIGHT MASCOT, AT IDRIS IN TRIPOLITANIA SHORTLY BEFORE THE UNIT BECAME 8 INDEPENDENT RECCE FLIGHT, ARMY AIR CORPS IN 1957.

of the war had shown that the helicopter was the obvious pretender to the Auster's AOP throne, even though the early machines were more expensive, more problematic to maintain and more prone to mechanical failure than the reliable old Auster. Indeed, while the discussions about the new AAC ranged back and forth, the Skeeter, destined to become the first helicopter in Army service, was struggling to rise higher than the mountain of paperwork that preceded its introduction.

When agreement was finally reached on the general form that the new Army Air Corps should take, it included a compromise to help define the roles to be undertaken by the Army in the air and the RAF's continuing responsibilities for air support. The Army Air Corps was to have control of

ABOVE: SKEETERS, SEEN HERE IN A WORKSHOP IN GERMANY, WERE INTENDED TO TAKE OVER MUCH OF THE AOP ROLE UNDERTAKEN BY THE AUSTER.

unarmed rotary and fixed wing aircraft not exceeding an all-up weight of 4000 lb. This basically meant that, from its inception, the Army Air Corps would be equipped with the Auster and, when they became available, the Skeeter for AOP, reconnaissance, light liaison and communications duties. The RAF would retain control of heavier aircraft and helicopters for ground support, troop transport and resupply. While this meant that the RAF's Austers would be transferred to the Army, it also meant that the Sycamores and Whirlwinds of the JEHU, being well above the 4000 lb weight limit, would ultimately join the RAF.

Once a general consensus had been reached, the task of establishing precisely how the Corps would be manned and funded fell to a staff officer at the War Office, Major (later Brigadier) R. A. Norman-Walker. As the RAF had previously been responsible for the procurement, maintenance and servicing of all aircraft (although the JEHU helicopters had been paid for by the Army) as well as the training of pilots and technical ground crew, a significant proportion of the personnel crucial to the running of the AAC were RAF. This was clearly not a situation that could be

changed in an instant. Norman-Walker canvassed support from various Army units in order to fulfil the requirement for the 1,500 officers and men that had been allocated to the Air Corps. At a time when it had been announced that National Service was to come to an end and manpower shortages were seen to be an ever-increasing problem, commanders were understandably reluctant to leave themselves undermanned by releasing personnel to a brand-new outfit. The AOP and Light Liaison units were, of course, operating all over the world with manpower in place, but the RAF staff would ultimately have to be withdrawn and many of the pilots would return to their parent units when their 'tour' as an Army flyer came to an end. For an Army officer especially, serving as a pilot was not seen as a desirable long-term career option.

With the help of expert advice from a number of officers already involved in Army flying, Norman-Walker laid out his plan for the organisation of the Air Corps. The Royal Air Force technical staff – the aircraft engineers and artificers – were to be replaced by REME personnel; the RAOC would supply the technical storemen and the Royal Signals, Royal Army Pay Corps and the Army

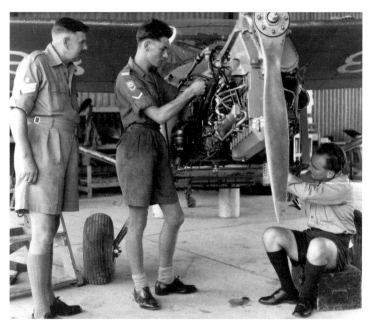

ABOVE: ARMY, NAVY AND AIR FORCE WORKING IN HARMONY AT NOBLE FIELD IN MALAYA, 1961.

BELOW: TRAINING WITH THE JEHU WARRANTED A SPECIALIST QUALIFICATION FOR RASC PERSONNEL OF HELICOPTER CREWMAN, THE FORERUNNER OF TODAY'S AIR TROOPER.

Catering Corps would all contribute personnel. The Royal Artillery, long having had a close relationship with Army flying, would continue to provide personnel for many of the non-technical ground posts as well as having a strong representation among the pilots. A permanent staff of forty-five AAC officers was established through the voluntary transfer of qualified pilots from all arms. The majority of the first quota of pilots came from the Royal Artillery but others were recruited from the RASC, the Royal Armoured Corps and the Infantry. Most pilots, whether officers or NCOs and from whatever branch of the military they originated, continued to be seconded for flying tours, at the end of which they returned to their parent units. The permanent cadre was there to provide the experience and continuity required to maintain and constantly improve upon the high professional standards expected of the AAC.

With so many different regiments involved, so many regimental loyalties to satisfy and a number of colonels who did not want to see their personnel, supplied on secondment, being surreptitiously subsumed within the new Corps, the thorny question of a regimental badge and uniform had to be addressed. While there were calls, especially among those of the former Glider Pilots Regiment, for the adoption of the airborne forces' maroon

1957 – 1967

ABOVE: FROM THE MID-FIFTIES ONWARDS THE CHIPMUNK WAS THE AIRCRAFT ON WHICH ARMY FLIERS RECEIVED THEIR INSTRUCTION.

RIGHT: JEHU TECHNICIANS HAD TO BE LITHE AND AGILE TO PERFORM MANY OF THE ROUTINE TASKS INVOLVED IN KEEPING THE SYCAMORES AND WHIRLWINDS FLYING.

beret, it was decided to opt for a new and different light blue hat. The regimental badge was first suggested by Major Bob Begbie. As Norman-Walker later wrote: 'The AAC eagle was first produced in the War Office by Bob Begbie in early 1957 – a drawing on tracing paper which I well remember. The present eagle may not be identical but I think that Bob has the right to claim it as his own.'

And he was welcome to keep it as his own, too, as far as some of the commanding officers of the parent regiments of many of the new recruits to the AAC were concerned. They wanted their men to wear their own berets and regimental badges. Norman-Walker recalled, 'The battle was only resolved by agreeing that

WESTLAND SCOUT AH MARK 1

SPECIFICATION

→ Engines	1 x Rolls Royce Nimbus 101 turboshaft
→ Maximum Level Flight Speed	131 mph
→ Cruising Speed	110 mph
→ Service Ceiling	17,700 feet
→ Armament	2 x 7.62 mm General Purpose Machine Guns 4 x Sud SS II guided missiles
→ Overall Length	40 feet 4 inches (12.29 m)
→ Height	8 feet 10 inches (2.7 m)
→ Main Rotor Span	32 feet 3 inches (9.83 m)
→ Maximum All-Up Weight	3100 lb (1409 kg)
→ Payload	1000 lb (454 kg)
→ Crew	1 pilot plus 1 crewman or up to four passengers

'...I HAD AN ENGINE FAILURE IN A SCOUT OVER THE BORNEO JUNGLE... IT WAS A BIT HAIRY ...'

MAJOR (RETD) TONY MARKHAM

The Scout was developed from the Sanders-Roe P 531 which, in turn, owed much to the design of the Skeeter. This led some to refer to the P 531 as a 'Super-Skeeter', although the Scout would go on to become a far more capable aircraft than the Skeeter. The P 531 first flew in September 1958. Technical difficulties meant that the first fully-fledged Scout did not take to the air until August 1960. Built by Westland's Fairey Division at Hayes in Middlesex, 149 Scouts were produced and the aircraft remained in service with the AAC until 1994.

The Scout has the honour of being the Army's first armed helicopter. Although it was used for casualty evacuation, carrying two stretchers outboard and two inside, amongst many other duties, the Scout was the aircraft which gave Army fliers the capability of striking at the enemy when it was fitted first with machine guns and later with anti-tank missiles. A maritime version of the Scout, the Wasp, was developed by Westland for the Royal Navy and had wheels rather than skids.

ABOVE: DURING ITS LIFETIME, THE BASE AT MIDDLE WALLOP WAS TO PLAY HOST TO THE RAF, THE ARMY AND THE NAVY AS WELL AS THE USAAF.

pilots should wear the blue beret with their regimental cap badge. Uniform sleeves were then to be decorated with sufficient titles and flashes, subject only to an ability to bend the elbow in salute, to signify the officer's parent Corps, present employment and, for all I can remember, marital status!'

For many of those already serving with the AOP squadrons, the change to AAC was not as disruptive as one might think. They had their jobs to do before the Air Corps was set up, and they had exactly the same jobs to do afterwards as well. Gunner Norman Langley was with 651 Squadron and recalled, 'Before, I was wearing my regimental badge, doing a bit of driving, aircraft handling, signalling, jack of all trades. Afterwards, I was doing the same thing. In between, we had a parade and congratulations all round.'

The Army Air Corps was established at Middle Wallop on 1 September 1957, giving the base the distinction of having been home to all three armed services. In the 1930s the RAF decided to site a bomber base on a grassy plateau lying to the east of the

Wallop Brook in Hampshire. The unusual name 'Wallop' refers not to any peculiar aircraft landing techniques that may have been practised in the area over the past seventy years, but is derived from the Old English words 'waella', meaning spring or stream, and 'hop' meaning valley. Middle Wallop is one of three villages strung out along the Wallop Brook, the others being Over Wallop, where the Wallop Brook rises, and Nether Wallop, downstream from Middle Wallop.

Work began on the new RAF base in 1938 and was nearing completion in 1940 when No. 15 Service Flying Training School moved down from Lossiemouth in Scotland. The base, therefore, has been associated with flying training from its earliest days. The flying school moved out a few months later when Middle Wallop became an important centre of operations during the Battle of

Britain. Hurricanes and Spitfires flew from the airfield and the base also became home to a night fighter squadron pioneering the use of airborne interception radar. The airfield did not escape the attentions of the Luftwaffe, suffering at least fourteen attacks between June 1940 and July 1941. The most severe of these came on 14 August 1940 when thirty Ju88s headed for Middle Wallop from their base in France. Twelve of the bombers made it as far as the airfield, one of them delivering a stick of four bombs which hit Hangar 5, destroying three Blenheims and killing three civilian workmen.

Middle Wallop saw a number of distinguished RAF squadrons come and go during the war years until, at the beginning of 1944, it was handed over to the United States Army Air Force who flew P-38 Lightnings and P-51 Mustangs on weather and photo-reconnaissance missions from the base. The Americans had moved on by August 1944 and the RAF resumed control of the base until February 1945 when Middle Wallop joined the Royal Navy. As HMS *Flycatcher*, RNAS Middle Wallop was used for the assembly of

ABOVE: THE OPERATIONS ROOM AT MIDDLE WALLOP, FROM WHERE ITS SECTOR'S FIGHTERS WERE DIRECTED TOWARDS ENEMY AIRCRAFT DURING THE BATTLE OF BRITAIN.

MONABs – Mobile Naval Air Operations Bases. MONABs were designed to be self-contained units that could be despatched to an airstrip anywhere in the world and quickly established to provide a forward repair base, servicing facilities, stores, training and rescue or liaison flights. The Navy made use of the base for less than a year before gratefully returning it to the RAF. By the spring of 1946, Middle Wallop was once more under the control of Fighter Command.

It was in January 1948 that the Austers of 657 Squadron AOP transferred from Andover to Middle Wallop, to be followed less than a fortnight later by 227 Operational Conversion Unit (formerly 43 OTU) whose job since 1940 had been to train artillery officers as AOP pilots. Thus began the Army's love affair with Middle Wallop. In 1950 the OCU was rechristened the AOP School and then the

'WHO TOLD THE BRIGADIER TO NAFF OFF?'

Light Aircraft School when it was merged with No. 22 Elementary Flying Training School. Middle Wallop was known as the Light Aircraft School until the Army Air Corps came into being in 1957 when the RAF sign on the main gate was changed to one that proclaimed the base to be the 'Army Air Corps Centre'.

Technically, Middle Wallop remained an RAF base for another year, and the RAF terminology used on site for the Pilot Training Wing and Technical Wing were retained, although the new commander of the facility held an Army rank – Brigadier, Army Air Corps. The first man to assume that title was Brigadier P.

sure enough, I heard, "Brigadier here." So I said, "Naff off", thinking it was one of my colleagues . . .

'Five minutes later, Buck Ryan, the Adjutant, came running in and said, "Who told the Brigadier to naff off?" I was shocked and replied, "Oh, God. It was me." The Adjutant told me that the Brigadier wanted to see me in his office at nine o'clock the following morning.

'I spent a sleepless night, sweating like mad, and the following morning I went into Buck's office at five to nine and waited nervously, until he said, "Okay, knock on the Brigadier's door and go

ABOVE: AN AUSTER MK 9 OF 21 FLIGHT IN UN COLOURS FLYING OVER TURKISH CYPRIOT POSITIONS IN HILARION CASTLE, CYPRUS IN 1964.

Weston, who had vast experience in RAF Army Co-operation Command both before and after the Second World War. Weston's new command was a maelstrom of activity, with REME personnel undergoing intensive training for their new roles and pilot training continuing apace. He could see that the workloads and pressure on his staff were becoming ever more extreme. Around this time, Freddie Legg (later to become Lt Col. Legg) remembers how, in lighter moments, the term 'Brigadier' came in for some unwarranted abuse. 'I was a flying instructor at Middle Wallop in 1957 and, after finishing a day's flying, I went into the instructor's crew room and the phone rang. Whenever it did, there was invariably someone on the other end mimicking the Brigadier and,

in." Feeling increasingly sick, I stepped inside and stood to attention, as the Brigadier was writing something on his desk. He didn't look up. He just kept me waiting there for quite some time. Eventually, he slowly raised his head and just said, "Naff orf!" And that was it!'

JEHU continued to be based at Middle Wallop, although the 'experimental' unit's Whirlwinds were once again to see active service when they were despatched to Cyprus in late 1958. The island had been a British protectorate since 1878, a Crown Colony since 1925 and of major military importance to the UK since the withdrawal from bases in Egypt in 1954. The vast majority of the population of Cyprus were of Greek extraction and, determined that they should not be ruled by a foreign government, they pressed for union with Greece. Around twenty per cent of the population, however, were of Turkish descent and strongly objected to the island becoming Greek. When the dispute turned to violent protest and insurrection, it was the Greek EOKA terrorists who became the major problem for the British authorities. Their bombing and assassination campaigns began in earnest in 1955, directed at British facilities and personnel. The British responded by hunting the terrorists down in their mountain hideaways.

The JEHU Whirlwinds were dismantled and loaded onto

ABOVE: DRAINING FUEL FROM AN AUSTER AT KHORMAKSAR IN ADEN IN 1962.

Beverley transport aircraft for the trip to Cyprus. There they joined the Auster AOP and Light Liaison flights that had been operating out of Nicosia, Lakatamia and Limassol since the emergency on the island began. They were to act as transport for a rapid reaction force and began training with a platoon from the Grenadier Guards. There were special rules to follow when flying in Cyprus. Flying was prohibited over the salt marshes to protect the flamingoes at Akrotiri and pilots were advised when flying over the Kyrenia mountains that they should 'Give way to eagles over high

ground'. But the local wildlife was not the only problem pilots had been obliged to deal with in Cyprus. Freddie Legg flew an Auster there in 1956. 'One of my favourite times was in Cyprus,' he remembered, 'but you really had to concentrate when landing on some of the very narrow air strips there. If you got a strong crosswind, it was sometimes almost beyond the Auster's capability. There was one particular air strip which had a steep bank on one side, and I remember seeing one aircraft running straight over the edge. Fortunately, no one was hurt, but that air strip certainly was an interesting challenge!'

'Challenge' certainly appeared to be a buzz word within the new Army Air Corps. The Royal Electrical and Mechanical

ABOVE: STARTING A SKEETER HAS ALWAYS BEEN AN ENTERTAINING BUSINESS . . .

Engineers had faced a tremendous challenge when they were required to take over responsibility from the RAF for the servicing and maintenance of the Army's aircraft. Within twelve months the REME were ready to do so, although until sufficient REME staff had been trained, RAF personnel would still be involved, and the Royal Navy provided staff on temporary secondment, too. Naval engineers were particularly keen to maintain their RN dress codes, including the right to grow beards, which led to some interesting scenes on parade, one squadron in Germany even providing a

ABOVE: MUCH ADMIRED NOT ONLY BY ITS PILOTS BUT ALSO BY THE GROUND CREWS, SEVENTEEN ALOUETTE IIS WERE ACQUIRED BETWEEN 1958 AND 1961.

visiting general with a naval quarterguard – white gaiters, cutlass and bo'sun's call never fail to impress.

The task of the REME was made even more formidable by the fact that the Army Air Corps was operating, like the rest of the Army, in a variety of different theatres from Northern Europe to the Far East. The organisational structure that was imposed called for two different types of AAC flight. Reconnaissance flights were structured to support a group of brigade strength, fulfilling the AOP role as well as providing tactical reconnaissance, aerial cable laying, courier and mail services. Liaison flights were required both as transport for unit commanders and to give them a first-hand reconnaissance capability. As well as these general communication and liaison duties, they were to provide casualty evacuation, transport limited amounts of specialist stores or equipment and perform signals support duties in cooperation with the recce flights. Independent flights were to be able to perform

both functions while supporting themselves in the field for indefinite periods. To accomplish all of these tasks, the AAC needed new types of aircraft, giving the REME crews even more on which to concentrate their minds.

The reliable old Austers, which had gradually been upgraded to the AOP Mk 9 with all-metal construction, were not best suited for passenger carrying and the new Skeeters could accommodate only one passenger. While the Skeeter had proved invaluable in providing experience in operating helicopters for everyone from ground crews to battlefield commanders, its limitations made it almost obsolete from its introduction. Neither was it entirely reliable. Starting the Skeeter's engine involved the use of a starter cartridge and to try to make sure that they could get their aircraft going during exercises on cold, damp mornings in Germany, pilots would often take the starter cartridge into their sleeping bags to make sure it remained warm and dry.

The Air Corps desperately needed more, and more modern, aircraft. Buying British had been politically desirable in the past, but the British replacement for the Skeeter, the Scout, was some way from going into production. As a stop-gap, seventeen Alouette

II helicopters were ordered between 1958 and 1961. The original version of the French Sud Aviation Alouette had broken helicopter speed and endurance records when it first flew in 1953. The Alouette II had improved upon those and claimed the altitude record to boot. Capable of carrying four passengers and operating anywhere in the world, it was exactly the kind of robust, versatile machine that the Air Corps required.

There was still, however, a requirement for a fixed-wing Auster replacement. This came in 1961 in the form of the Canadian-built de Havilland Beaver AL Mk 1. The Beaver could accommodate five passengers and was a rugged aircraft originally designed to operate in remote areas. With a maximum all-up weight of over 5000 lb, the Beaver consigned the 4000 lb rule for Army machines to the scrapheap. The Austers were not, of course, banished from the Corps straight away. Some aircraft were still in use up to 1966, the marque having contributed over twenty-five years of loyal service to the Army.

If Army flying was fast becoming a very serious business, that message had yet to seep through to some of its aviators. Major (Retd) Peter Elgar remembers enjoying himself immensely in the

ABOVE: THE BEAVER PROVIDED STERLING SERVICE THROUGHOUT THE YEARS OF THE CONFLICT IN ADEN.

AAC. 'In 1964 I was at Middle Wallop doing trial and development. I would fly four or five aircraft a day – mainly helicopters – and that was great fun. Prior to that I was in Germany where there was a great camaraderie.

'I would regularly fly home from Germany to go to friends' parties, stay overnight and then fly back. You would get court martialled for that sort of thing now! I remember one occasion I flew to my parents' house and landed on their lawn. My mother got into the plane and we took off. She was terribly excited. The neighbours were saying, "Look, there's Roz in the plane with Peter." She never forgot that.'

Captain (later Major) Neil Baldwick also managed to put an AAC machine to use in a manner for which it was never intended. 'In 1959, when I was in 651 Squadron,' he recalls, 'I sought permission to enter the prestigious King's Cup Air Race and I was told that I could, on condition that any prize money I received went to the MOD and that I paid the entrance fee myself. So we entered

ABOVE: THE ALOUETTES OF 653 SQUADRON WERE DIVERTED TO KENYA WHEN THE SQUADRON WAS DEPLOYED TO ADEN IN 1960.

a Mk6 Auster – a bit like a bicycle frame covered in canvas – and got a team of REME technicians to work on it in their spare time. It was the first time any military aircraft had been entered.

'They streamlined the airframe and replaced the propeller with a more efficient one from a Chipmunk. We took it up and did some time trials and found that we could get over 100 knots out of it. Whereas 70–75 was average.

'We spent a week in Coventry where the event took place, doing the heats first and then the final. You take off from the airfield, at staggered intervals, according to the handicap system, and you fly five laps round a rectangular 20-mile course, with a pylon on each corner and an observer who would check that you were going around the pylon. And it's first home. There were about six aircraft in the final and I came second. But I did become British

National Air Racing Champion.'

Needless to say, there was plenty of military activity to keep the Corps busy throughout this period as well. In addition to the continuing commitment to BAOR, in Malaya and in Cyprus, elements of the Air Corps were also deployed in Kenya during the latter part of the Mau Mau Emergency in 1960 where they also became involved in flood and famine relief; in Kuwait when Iraq threatened to invade in 1961; in Borneo during the conflict with Indonesia from 1962 to 1967; in British Guiana during the pre-independence disturbances in 1964; in East Africa during the mutinies there in 1964; and in Aden from 1960 to 1967 when terrorists and hill tribesmen wrought havoc prior to the British departure from the former colony.

Having been disbanded at the end of the Second World War, 653 Squadron was reformed in Cyprus in 1958. In 1960 its Austers and Alouettes moved to Aden (although the Alouettes were then transferred to Kenya) and by 1964, when concerted

ABOVE: IN 1963, ARMY AIR CORPS ALOUETTES FLEW BREAD AND OTHER ESSENTIAL SUPPLIES TO VILLAGERS IN THE SOUTH OF ENGLAND CUT OFF BY THE WORST SNOWSTORMS FOR OVER EIGHTY YEARS.

BELOW: UNRULY UNAUTHORISED PERSONNEL ON PARADE IN KENYA IN 1964.

AUGUSTA-BELL SIOUX AH MARK 1

SPECIFICATION

→ Engines	1 x Avco Lycoming TVO-435-B1A
→ Maximum Level Flight Speed	105 mph
→ Cruising Speed	86 mph
→ Service Ceiling	20,000 feet
→ Armament	1 x 7.62 mm General Purpose Machine Gun occasionally mounted on landing gear front cross member
→ Overall Length	40 feet (12.19 m)
→ Height	9 feet 4 inches (2.84 m)
→ Main Rotor Span	37 feet 1 inch (9.78 m)
→ Maximum All-Up Weight	2950 lb (1341 kg)
→ Payload	Two stretchers could be mounted outboard on skids
→ Crew	1 pilot plus two passengers

Unfortunately, the Sioux was not quite as trouble-free as the Army had expected it to be. Potential problems, especially with the engine's turbo charger, were swiftly overcome by REME engineers to ensure that the Sioux, nicknamed 'the clockwork mouse' because it had the frail appearance of a child's toy, became a highly reliable aircraft. It went on to prove its worth on operations in environments as diverse as Northern Ireland and Borneo or Cyprus and Belize.

The Sioux started life in 1945 as the Bell 47, around the same time as the Skeeter, and entered military service with the US Army in 1946. Built under licence by Augusta in Italy and later Westland at their Yeovil plant, over 200 Sioux served with the AAC over two decades from 1964 onwards. Intended as a direct replacement for the Skeeter, the Sioux performed a multitude of tasks, even becoming the first aircraft to be used by the AAC Blue Eagles helicopter display team when they first formed in 1968.

ABOVE: AN RAF BELFAST UNLOADS ITS CARGO OF SIOUX AT SHARJAH.

efforts to thwart the Communist-backed insurgents crossing into Aden from Yemen were under way, the Squadron had added the Beaver and the Scout to its inventory. Developed from the Saunders-Roe P 531 the aircraft became the Westland Scout AH Mk 1 (Westland having taken over Saunders-Roe) when it entered service with the AAC in 1963. Powered by a Rolls-Royce Nimbus, the Scout could lift a payload of 1000 lb or carry up to four passengers. Capable of operating under any climatic conditions,

this was the helicopter for which the Army had been waiting and it was to change the nature of Army aviation entirely.

Although still undergoing 'hot and high' flying trials in Aden, the first Scouts were quickly involved in lifting SAS patrols into the mountains from their forward base at Thumier, just thirty miles from the Yemeni border. Traversing the hill country, the Scouts regularly came under fire from snipers hidden among the rocks, as did the Beavers when they flew recce missions or dropped supplies to troops in the mountains. Neither were they safe when on the ground. Neil Baldwick recalls presenting himself as a tempting target. 'I have a very vivid memory of nearly being shot by our own men in Aden. The army was fighting dissident tribesmen, up country, in the mountains. We were the support and so we decided to move from our base to stay with them.

'We slept in bivouacs inside the wire perimeter. That was an interesting experience because, at night, the rebels outside would shoot at us. So we built little stone walls around our bivouacs so that when we lay down, our heads and bodies were below the wall.

'They would still take pot shots at us, though, and a guard would send up some flares for illumination and it would all quieten down. Many of us used to sleep in Arab sarongs and I remember one night I was awoken by a hell of a commotion. Up went the

LEFT: AFTER EARLY ENGINE TEETHING TROUBLES LONG-AWAITED SCOUT PROVED TO BE EVERYTHING THE AAC HAD HOPED FOR.

flares. I grabbed my 9mm Browning and walked around, wondering what was going on. The rebels were trying to get through the wire and suddenly it dawned on me that I looked just like one of them. I was lucky not to be shot!'

Having Army crews operating the support helicopters proved its worth in Aden in many ways, not least when it came to resupplying 3 Para, who were operating on the Bakri ridge, the Jebel Haqla and in the Wadi Dhubsan in June 1964. Water and ammunition were their key requirements and knowing where to drop the supplies was vital. During the course of one hour, one AAC Scout made enough trips into the mountains to deliver three times the load carried by an RAF twin-rotor Belvedere, which boasted six times the Scout's payload capacity. Moreover, the Scout delivered the supplies to a site indicated by the men on the ground, whereas the Belvedere pilot chose to land the supplies at a spot that best suited him. For the Paras, this meant a great deal of arduous load carrying over rough terrain in intense heat – hugely counter-productive when water was such a precious commodity.

With the Scouts providing a shuttle service to supply water, food and ammunition as well as evacuating casualties on their return trip, the Paras made rapid advances. In one report they claimed to have captured so much ground that their CO asked to be flown in to verify their position. Unfortunately, the Scout proved to be too tempting a target for the enemy snipers hidden on the hillsides and took several hits. One of the CO's party was wounded and the aircraft was in trouble. The pilot, Major Jake Jackson, managed to make a landing close to a less hotly contested 3 Para outpost and REME technician Corporal Carcarry was flown in to assess the damage. Having compiled a list of necessary replacement parts he was then lifted back to Thumier by Scout then on to Little Aden some sixty miles distant by Auster. Although the damaged Scout was in no danger of being overrun by the enemy, the aircraft was now a sitting duck for the snipers who

BELOW: A SCOUT WITH AN ARMOURED FERRET SCOUT CAR IN ADEN IN 1964.

ABOVE: CAPTAIN R. GREVATTE-BALL AT SHARJAH IN 1967 WITH HIS BEAVER BEARING THE UNOFFICIAL 'BLACK CAT' BADGE OF 13 FLIGHT.

would close in under cover of darkness and do some real damage in the morning. After collecting the spares from Little Aden, Corporals Carcarry and Hustwith were delivered back to the Wadi before dark and then worked through the night, by torchlight under blanket black-out covers, to make the repairs. At first light, the Scout was fired up, ran under test and flew back to Thumier without a hiccup. The incident was one among many to prove the serviceability of the Scout and the undoubted skill of the REME in the field.

The AAC was involved in Aden until the final withdrawal from the territory in 1967 but, while the situation in Aden was unfolding, another drama was being played out thousands of miles to the east on the island of Borneo. In December 1962 rebels backed by Indonesia, which controlled the territory known as Kalimantan that covered half the island, launched a coup attempt against the Sultan of Brunei. The oil-rich state of Brunei lay on the northern coast of Borneo between the British colonies of Sarawak and North Borneo (both soon to be independent with North Borneo becoming Sabah). The Sultan appealed to Britain for help and, although unprepared for their deployment, the Gurkhas, Royal Marines, Green Jackets and Queen's Own Highlanders,

amongst others, were hurriedly despatched to Borneo from Singapore to be joined by Austers, Beavers and a handful of helicopters from 656 Squadron, based at Kluang in Malaysia. The squadron was sorely stretched to provide much support for the RAF and Royal Navy aircraft operating in Borneo. 'I was sent out to the Far East to be what was rather grandly called Commander of Army Aviation, Borneo,' recalled Major John Dicksee. 'In fact, what I commanded was a Land-Rover and two soldiers!'

Major Dicksee's responsibilities were to increase dramatically when, in mid-1964 656 Squadron was reinforced with sixteen Scouts and its CO, Lt Col. Bob Begbie was able to increase his operational commitment to Borneo to two helicopter flights and a fixed wing detachment. The Austers and Beavers were essential in providing the most cost-effective reconnaissance and passenger transport but it was the helicopters which ultimately allowed a relatively small number of men on the ground to gain control of the 1300 miles of mountainous jungle that formed the border with Kalimantan. The Scouts operated from Kuching in Sarawak,

ABOVE: 656 SQUADRON STORES ARE UNLOADED AT BRUNEI IN
DECEMBER 1962.

RIGHT: TONY MARKHAM WAS TO HAVE SOME CLOSE CALLS FLYING HIS
SCOUT IN BORNEO.

from Brunei and from Long Pa Sia in Sabah.

Sergeant (later Major) Tony Markham had joined the AAC from
the Royal Signals for a three-year tour in 1964. He trained on the
Scout at Middle Wallop before being posted to Kluang for theatre
conversion training and then on to Long Pa Sia to join 11 Flight. He
would have good cause to be grateful for the training that was
drummed into him at Middle Wallop and Kluang. 'Flying technique
helped to save my life, as well as my passengers, in 1965 when I had
an engine failure in a Scout over the Borneo jungle,' he maintained.
'I had a party of officers from the Royal Green Jackets aboard who
had carried out a recce for operations. We had just left a helipad
that had been created on the top of a mountain, to go back to base,
when the engine quit. It was caused by a fuel line breaking free.

'I was about 3,000 feet up but unable to get back onto the

helipad. It was a bit hairy because in Borneo, each tree is about 250 feet high and all the branches are at the top, there is nothing lower down. If you crash into them, you have a dead fall of over 200 feet. So, knowing the survival chances were slim, I tried to stretch the glide as far as I could.

'I did a series of hops and dives over the mountain ridges until eventually I couldn't get over one because it was too high. So I turned along it and, in doing so, I found, within gliding range, a patch of green which was lighter in colour to its surroundings. It turned out to be a rain water collecting point, with bamboo and grasses and small trees, which were much easier to land in.

'I managed to get to the area and then stood the helicopter on its tail and descended. The tail absorbed a lot of the impact and, although it was a heavy landing and the aircraft broke quite badly,

LEFT: WATER DELIVERIES COURTESY OF A SCOUT IN ADEN IN 1964.

BELOW: AAC HELICOPTERS PLAYED A LARGE PART IN WINNING THE 'HEARTS AND MINDS' OF LOCAL PEOPLE SUCH AS THE EBAN IN BORNEO.

one person on board jarred his back but everyone else was fine.'

Markham recalls the base at Long Pa Sia being a rough and ready affair. 'Long Pa Sia had a grass landing strip capable of accepting Beaver, Scout, Single and Twin Pioneer aircraft only, and became waterlogged during the monsoon season. The six Scouts were perched inside the barbed wire entanglements beside the strip on log platforms to give some eighteen inches' clearance from the ground. This also seemed to keep snakes and rats away from the aircraft, besides keeping them above flood water level.

'We were responsible for our own sector of the defensive perimeter and stood-to at first and last light in bunkers connected by a trench system similar to World War I. The main defensive position was guarded by the Gurkhas whom we were to transport out to patrol points, resupply and recover continuously, being some three grid squares from the Kalimantan border.'

Flying in close proximity to the border meant that the aircraft regularly came under small-arms and anti-aircraft fire from the Indonesian side. To give them a chance of hitting back, Markham remembers that, '. . . fixed, forward firing machine guns were fitted to the Scouts . . .' Similar experiments had been tried in England and, although the machine guns were far from accurate, they helped to keep the enemy's heads down. More importantly, the first steps had now been taken towards arming Army aircraft.

When later flying out of Kuching, Sergeant Markham was one of the Army pilots who became heavily involved in ferrying SAS patrols to jungle LZs from where they would cross the border on missions inside Kalimantan. This was highly dangerous work and his expertise was very much appreciated by the special forces soldiers, who came to regard him almost as one of their own. In fact, when an Ausralian SAS unit was handing over to D Squadron SAS, they kidnapped him! He was roused from his basha in the middle of the night and taken to the SAS HQ, where, rather than being briefed for another sortie, he found a loud hand-over party in full swing. 'I explained that I had a sortie planned for seven o'clock that morning but was told I had been relieved of all duties until they had finished with me . . .' The party rolled on through swimming and volleyball matches the next day . . . and the day

ABOVE: FORWARD FIRING MACHINE GUNS WERE FITTED TO SCOUTS FOR SELF DEFENCE, BUT SERGEANT BRAZIER FOUND HIS DOOR MOUNTING MORE ACCURATE.

after. 'I was eventually delivered back to Airport Camp at night on the third day convinced that I would be court martialled, but my OC completely ignored the whole incident!'

While the Scout, after a few early engine teething troubles, was providing sterling service to the AAC, by 1964 the Skeeter was showing its age. Replacing the Skeeter fleet with the more expensive Scout was not financially viable, so an alternative light helicopter was sought. The eventual choice was the Augusta-Bell 47-G3-B1, originally designed by the American Bell Helicopter company, early versions had been in service with the US military since 1946 and its distinctive bubble canopy is easily recognised by anyone familiar with the *M.A.S.H.* movie and TV series. Augusta-Bell manufactured the aircraft under licence in Italy from where the first of the AAC machines were imported before Westland also

'I WAS EVENTUALLY DELIVERED BACK TO AIRPORT CAMP
AT NIGHT ON THE THIRD DAY CONVINCED THAT
I WOULD BE COURT MARTIALLED . . .'

acquired a licence to build what became known as the Sioux AH Mk 1 when it entered AAC service.

Other ways of providing cost-effective aerial reconnaissance were also investigated, although some were less successful than others. Major (Retd) Time Deane remembers trying one such machine. 'If you have ever seen the movie *You Only Live Twice* with James Bond skilfully manoeuvring in an autogyro, well, let me tell you, my experience was very different!

ABOVE: AN RAF HASTINGS TRANSPORT DWARFS THE AUSTERS ON THE RUNWAY AT KUCHING.

BELOW LEFT: CORPORAL WOOD WITH RNAS 845 SQUADRON PET MUSANG, A TYPE OF CIVET, CAUGHT AT NANJA GAAT, INSPECTING AN AUSTER.

BELOW RIGHT: ROSEMARY SKINNER, WIFE OF 845 SQUADRON PILOT BRIAN SKINNER HELPS OUT WITH A LEAFLET DROP OVER SIBU.

'In 1961 I was in the Royal Artillery and was one of three pilots chosen to do flight trials in a Wallace-Benson Autogyro. It was the WA116 – a prototype of the one seen in the Bond movie. It may look glamorous on the big screen but the reality of it is like sitting in a dining room chair, thousands of feet in the air!

'The MOD had bought three or four of these gyros to see if they were suitable for army aerial reconnaissance. They cost £846 each and I reduced two of them to matchwood! They were neither aeroplane nor helicopter but a machine with a rotor blade and so they took some getting used to. You sat on a chair with the main body of the gyro strapped to your back. It had very little payload which meant that the pilots had to be quite light and there was no radio, because it would have been too heavy. There wasn't much else except for an engine, an altimeter and a stick that you moved to turn sideways.

'On my first flight I was flying over a ploughed field when the engine failed and I made an emergency landing. The thing had tiny wheels – like castor wheels – and toppled over when I hit the ground. I got up, with the thing still strapped to my back, and saw a ploughman waving at me, looking totally bemused.

'The second occasion was when I was supporting an Army manoeuvre – an amphibious landing in Cornwall. The engine failed as I was looming over a cliff and I landed on the beach, rolled over two or three times and came to a halt, upside down, right in front of the leading members of the assault team. One of them said, "Realistic here, isn't it?"'

The autogyro was rejected, just as it had been thirty years before, but the ever-expanding role of the AAC now required them to look to the future to develop new ways of using their aircraft, and the exciting new aircraft under development, to leave behind the Corps' image as a pure support arm and go on the offensive.

BELOW: THE SIOUX PROVED TO BE A HIGHLY RELIABLE AIRCRAFT, DESPITE HAVING BEEN DESIGNED AT THE SAME TIME AS THE SKEETER.

CHAPTER FIVE

CHANGES IN THE AIR
1967 – 1977

The ever-changing nature of Army aviation, fuelled by the ongoing development of new technology, has meant that, ever since its inception in 1957, the AAC has had to be prepared to adapt to circumstances as they evolved. The most obvious manifestation of this necessary flexibility has been in the training and retraining of personnel in the use of new equipment. Ground crews must learn how to deploy and maintain new vehicles, new weapons systems and new aircraft, acquiring new skills that keep pace with the constant learning curve faced by pilots and aircrew.

The need for adaptability, however, applies not only to the men and women at the 'sharp end' of Army flying. The organisational structure of the AAC has undergone several reviews since the Corps was founded in 1957.

The first re-organisation of the AAC came about in the early 1960s when the 'Integration' policy was adopted. This was a very logical extension of the reasoning that had led to the establishment of the AAC in the first place. The Army needed to have control of its air assets to put them to best use, therefore the AAC had come into being. In order that individual units could then utilise the air arm most effectively, it followed that they should have more direct control. The Integration policy allowed that if a commander in the field needed a helicopter or observation aircraft, he should be able to order its deployment as easily as he could whistle up a Land-Rover. Units would form their own air arms ready to meet the specific needs of their own commanders.

In 1963, the long-term plan for integration was put into practice, the first phase involving the creation of twenty-eight new flights – thirteen to serve with the Royal Armoured Corps, eleven with the Royal Artillery, two with the Royal Engineers and two with the Infantry. The overall plan was intended to help save on manpower as the 'parent' units would ultimately supply their own pilots and ground crews to be trained at Middle Wallop. A further two phases of the plan would be brought into effect over the coming years, spreading the provision of aircraft to even more Army units. The Royal Artillery referred to their air elements as 'Air OP Troops', the Infantry as 'Air Platoons', the Royal Armoured Corps as 'Air Squadrons' or 'Air Troops', the Royal Signals and Royal Engineers also adopting the name 'Air Troop'.

LEFT: AN ALOUETTE SITS ON A LANDING PAD OF IMMACULATELY-PAINTED WHITE STONES ATTENDED BY TWO IMMACULATELY-PAINTED WHITE FERRET SCOUT CARS ON UN DUTIES IN CYPRUS.

ABOVE: ALL AAC AIRCRAFT PRACTISE DECK LANDINGS ABOARD CARRIERS OR SUPPORT SHIPS AND THIS ALOUETTE IS SEEN ON THE DECK OF HMS *BULWARK* IN THE ENGLISH CHANNEL. THIS IS NOT THE MODERN AMPHIBIOUS ASSAULT SHIP *BULWARK* BUT HER PREDECESSOR, A LIGHT FLEET CARRIER SCRAPPED IN 1984.

While the integration scheme was intended to help address the growing problem of personnel shortages within the AAC at a time when the Army as a whole was undergoing the endemic phenomenon of manpower cutbacks, there were many who disagreed with the integration concept as a whole. John Dicksee saw two recce helicopter sections from his squadron sent to Germany to participate in integration trials with an artillery regiment and a field engineer regiment. In a later report on the trials he noted that, '. . . from an aviation point of view the trials revealed nothing new. We already knew the value of affiliations with supported units, and the deployment of aircraft "in direct support" or "under command" were well tried procedures inherited by the AAC from AOP, so any experienced AAC flight or squadron commander could have written the report without doing the trial!'

Dicksee further noted that following the establishment of integrated unit flights, '. . . the AAC squadrons on which our esprit de corps had been founded were now virtually demolished. In effect, "integration" meant "disintegration" as far as the AAC was concerned. Our administrative manpower was removed in the interests of economy and divisional flights were absorbed into the establishments of their respective headquarters and signals squadrons. They became "parasitic", as the official rationale for this ploy described it, and their helicopters became a "pool" for headquarters use – phrases hardly likely to inspire. My own reaction was that I had not transferred to a new and exciting corps to be relegated to a parasitic pool.'

Dicksee was not alone in his criticism of the Integration programme. There were many who were loath to see the Air Corps reduced to little more than a training organisation providing support and advice to other Army units. As valuable as this role might be, it was not how many of its permanent cadre had seen the future of the AAC. The true enthusiasts of Army aviation had imagined that the AAC would gradually assume a far more pro-active role on the battlefield, expanding their duties in observation and communication to include a combat capability. That, in fact, was indirectly to become one of the deciding factors in the revision of Integration.

Arming Scouts with machine guns in Borneo and Aden, even dropping bombs from Beavers, had shown how the Air Corps could contribute a strike capability in a combat situation. The British

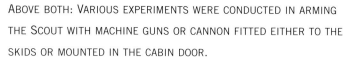

ABOVE BOTH: VARIOUS EXPERIMENTS WERE CONDUCTED IN ARMING THE SCOUT WITH MACHINE GUNS OR CANNON FITTED EITHER TO THE SKIDS OR MOUNTED IN THE CABIN DOOR.

RIGHT: THE SCOUT CARRIED FOUR SS11 WIRE-GUIDED ANTI-TANK MISSILES, THE SIGHTING SYSTEM FOR THE MISSILES MOUNTED ON THE ROOF OF THE COCKPIT.

Army was, to a great degree, lagging behind its allies in the area of armed helicopter development. The French had armed their helicopters during their Algerian campaign in the 1950s to provide suppressive fire when disembarking troops in forward positions. The Americans had begun to develop 'helicopter gunships' in Vietnam. It was clear that the helicopter was evolving into an offensive weapon and in Germany, the British Army identified a clear need for such a capability.

While the Cold War stalemate endured along the border between East and West Germany, the overwhelming numbers of

Warsaw Pact tanks ranged against the Western powers' defensive lines gave serious cause for concern. Should the WP launch a conventional attack, their tactics would be to punch a hole through the Western defences, advancing rapidly by using their superior numbers to sweep aside defending allied tanks. They

ABOVE: ARMING AND REFUELLING A SCOUT AT A FARP (FORWARD
ARMING AND REFUELLING POINT) ON EXERCISE ON SALISBURY PLAIN.

LEFT: AN SS11 FRACTIONS OF A SECOND AFTER BEING FIRED, WITH
THE WIRE FOR THE GUIDANCE SYSTEM CLEARLY VISIBLE AS IT REELS
OUT BEHIND.

would then push on westward, expanding their advance, preventing the NATO armies from reorganising or establishing a fresh line of defence. Delaying the WP advance until more armoured units could be brought into play required a swift and agile response. The helicopter was seen as one possible solution.

In 1964, extensive trials began with Scouts armed with French SS11 guided missiles. The SS11 was a wire-guided missile, a thin control wire reeling out as the missile headed towards its target. The operator could 'fly' the missile remotely, using a joystick to send adjustment commands along the control wire, keeping it on track. The SS11 had been in service with the French since 1956 and with the Americans since 1961, so had a proven track record, although directing it on to its target was a highly skilled job. Taking part in exercises in Germany, SS11-armed Scouts were pitted against tanks and low-level air defence systems, where they proved that the helicopter was a highly effective tank buster.

DE HAVILLAND BEAVER AL MK 1

'SOLID AND RELIABLE, IT'S BEEN DESCRIBED AS ONE OF THE BEST INVESTMENTS THE BRITISH ARMY EVER MADE'.

LT COL BILL WRIGHT, BEAVER PILOT AND LEADER OF THE AAC HISTORIC AIRCRAFT FLIGHT

The De Havilland company of Canada took on a mighty task when they decided to create an aircraft that would be ideal for Canadian backwoods pilots. The machine had to be strong enough to operate from the roughest of landing areas using wheels, skis or floats. It had to be able to take off from short strips in forest clearings and be easy to maintain in the field. Needless to say, it also had to be able to accommodate a useful payload. The Beaver met all of the criteria and, from the moment the first prototype took to the air in 1947, it was a clear winner. The US Army was to order almost 1,000 Beavers over the years, over half of the entire lifetime production run, although the aircraft was also sold to a number of other military operators in sixty-two countries around the world.

The Beaver entered service with the AAC in 1961, for deployment throughout the world, including Borneo and Aden as well as on its home territory at BATUS and in Northern Ireland where it became the Army's primary surveillance platform. An Army Beaver was attached to the British Embassy in Laos in the late sixties and others performed near miracles during civil assistance operations, supplying equipment for the building of roads and bridges in the Sudan and Ethiopia in the seventies. Over forty Beavers were to serve with the AAC up to their gradual replacement by the Islander in the late eighties.

SPECIFICATION

→ Engines	1 x Pratt & Whitney R-985 Wasp Jr. radial engine, 450 hp (335 kW)
→ Maximum Level Flight Speed	158 mph
→ Service Ceiling	18,000 feet (5486 m)
→ Range	455 miles
→ Armament	None normally
→ Overall Length	30 feet 3 inches (9.22 m)
→ Height	9 feet (2.74 m)
→ Wingspan	48 feet (14.63 m)
→ Weight	3,000 lb (1360 kg)
→ Payload	2,100 lb (950 kg)
→ Crew	1 pilot plus up to 6 passengers

With the AAC's helicopters moving on from carrying the sort of 'defensive' armament used in Aden and Borneo to adopting a new 'offensive' role using what were envisaged to become ever more complex weapons systems, the time had come to re-evaluate 'integration'. Although units such as the Queen's Dragoon Guards had demonstrated in training manoeuvres that they could operate far more effectively with their own 'air troop', keeping small and diverse detachments airborne was proving to be a logistical nightmare. Dispersal of the Army's aircraft among so many different units was putting a severe strain on the resources of the REME and there were now new Army helicopters on the drawing board with new weapons systems all of which would require highly specialised skills in their maintenance and operation. The advantages of Integration were becoming overwhelmed by the logistical problems of deploying aircraft to regimental level.

True to form, the AAC demonstrated its flexibility once more in 1967 when proposals were drawn up to reorganise the Corps at a time when the previous integration plan had yet to be fully implemented. The new order of battle was to encompass the equivalent of twenty squadrons – actually eighteen squadrons and five independent flights. Although continuing to operate from bases all over world – Hong Kong, Libya, Cyprus, the Persian Gulf, Germany and the UK – the AAC's aircraft were to be reclaimed in their own regiments and squadrons under a unified command structure. Only the Royal Armoured Corps armoured car and reconnaissance regiments retained their own air squadrons, although these would also ultimately return to the AAC once more.

The new structure called for a staffing level of 2,771 officers and other ranks, almost twice the strength of the fledgling AAC in 1957. Of this number almost half were to be REME personnel – 68 officers

BELOW: THIS SCOUT HAS BEEN FITTED WITH EXPERIMENTAL FLOTATION AIDS TO HELP KEEP THE AIRCRAFT ON THE SURFACE LONG ENOUGH FOR THE CREW TO ABANDON SHIP SHOULD THEY HAVE TO DITCH OVER WATER.

ABOVE: BETWEEN THEM THE SCOUT AND THE SIOUX WOULD GIVE FORTY-FIVE YEARS' SERVICE TO THE AAC.

and 1,263 other ranks. Just as had happened when the Corps was first formed, of course, many soldiers simply carried on doing the job they had been trained to do. And, just as had also happened previously, commanders of other units were outraged when their personnel were seconded for service with the AAC. There were many advantages to having personnel 'on loan' from other units. It brought fresh ideas to the AAC and helped to maintain strong contacts with many different regiments but, especially with so much specialised new equipment being introduced, continuity of service was now seen as being paramount. Having experienced men in technical posts was becoming vital but it was no less important to have soldiers with experience in aircraft marshalling and refuelling, or operating the fire and crash services, or working in air traffic control. The soldiers who worked on the ground had also, in the past, been called upon to earn the special 'half wings' they received when they completed their training as air observers and now there would also be a requirement for air gunners. Obviously, the AAC

would lose such staff who were on temporary secondment when they were reclaimed by their parent units and the only way to maintain a continuity of skills was to make such postings permanent appointments. To achieve this, the AAC needed to be able to recruit from outside the Army.

In 1973 the Army Air Corps was instituted as a Fighting Arm alongside the Royal Armoured Corps and the Infantry. The Scout, with its tank-busting missiles, had transformed the AAC by adding an offensive capability to the many other roles undertaken by the Corps. Also around this period, direct entry into the AAC became possible for the first time. Anyone looking towards a career in the Army could now enlist in the AAC, wearing the blue beret and cap badge of the Corps. Soldiers could enlist for general or clerical duties and the opportunity existed for them to progress to pilot training if they had the desire and aptitude to do so. On enlisting, the private soldier was given the new title of Air Trooper. Officers could now join the AAC direct from the Royal Military Academy on

ABOVE: THE SCOUT SAW SERVICE IN THE FORMER BRITISH COLONY OF BELIZE WHEN NEIGHBOURING GUATEMALA BEGAN TO THREATEN THE TERRITORY IN 1975. BELIZE REMAINS A FAVOURITE SUNSHINE POSTING FOR AAC PERSONNEL.

direct recruiting in 1973,' he recalls, 'and the first to reach the rank of Lt Col from Air Trooper.

'I wanted to fly and the AAC offered direct entry and it has given me the opportunity to fly all sorts of aircraft, both helicopters and fixed wing. Today, I am part of the Military Aviation Regulatory Team working out of Yeovilton, who are responsible for flight regulations within the services but I've done all sorts of things in the AAC – air gunner, pilot, flight commander.'

No such achievements, of course, come without a great deal of dedication and hard work. The new breed of AAC soldier, in fact, had to develop skills reminiscent of those displayed by the men of the old Glider Pilot Regiment – pilots in the air but infantrymen on the ground. For all of the soldiers who were to enlist in the AAC, the increasing complexity of the equipment they were to handle meant that they needed to have the capacity to learn new skills. As Bill Wright put it: 'In any job there will be times where you ask questions of yourself. You might not like what you are doing, or things become a bit challenging, but my advice to younger recruits is that it is all do-able. I mean, I've done it. I was a late entry commission in 1990 and became Lt Col in February '97. I've got no regrets. I've enjoyed everything I have done. If you stick at it, you can go places.'

either regular or short-service commissions while opportunities were increased for non-commissioned officers to train as pilots. Prior to the new reorganisation, there were twice as many pilots on secondment doing their three-year tour of duty as there were pilots in permanent postings. This ratio was to be reversed.

Bill Wright was an early beneficiary of the new recruitment programme. 'I was one of the first to join the AAC after we started

While organisation and reorganisation continued, of course, the AAC still had commitments to fulfil all over the world. 1967 saw Britain finally withdraw from Aden, where the AAC had been so heavily involved. Part of the MOD's Defence Estimates report in 1968 paid tribute to the flyers in South Arabia, stating that, 'Aircrews of all three Services effectively assisted our troops . . . Helicopters of the Royal Navy, Royal Air Force and the Army Air

'. . . THE ARMY AIR CORPS WERE A BOON FOR THE SWEATING GROUND TROOPS . . . SAVING LIFE BY QUICKLY MOVING CASUALTIES TO HOSPITAL.'

ABOVE: A CURIOUS GROUP OF MASAI TRIBESPEOPLE EXAMINE A SIOUX
ON EXERCISE IN KENYA IN 1975.

RIGHT: CAPTAIN JOHN ALLEN POSES WITH HIS SIOUX ON MOUNT KENYA
AT 14,000 FEET.

Corps were a boon to the sweating ground troops seeking out
dissident gangs, carrying soldiers to posts on craggy heights and
saving life by quickly moving casualties to hospital.'

Aden had been a hugely important proving ground for the
effectiveness of the Scout operating in support of Army patrols but
at home in Britain, the Army's helicopters were also showing how
effectively they could master a range of vital roles. In March 1967
a special flight of three AAC Sioux flying out of the Netheravon
base embarked on a series of trials for the Home Office, working
with the police to help evaluate the use of helicopters in police
work. Judging by the number of helicopters in service with police
authorities all over Britain today, the Home Office must have

1967 – 1977

deemed those initial trials a success!

Also in March 1967, AAC helicopters were used to aid the civil authorities when the Torrey Canyon oil tanker foundered on rocks between the Scilly Isles and Land's End. A massive slick of 31 million gallons of oil contaminated 60 miles of coastline in France and 120 miles of the Cornish coast. Troops joined civilian volunteers in spraying the beaches with detergent to disperse the oil, AAC helicopters helping to deliver drums of detergent to the clean-up teams.

On a lighter note, in the spring of 1968, the AAC was able to showcase its talent in a most spectacular manner when the Blue Eagles helicopter display team was formed. As well as

ABOVE: FIRST FORMED IN 1968, THE AAC BLUE EAGLES HELICOPTER DISPLAY TEAM WAS ORIGINALLY MANNED BY ENTHUSIASTIC VOLUNTEERS WHO GAVE UP THEIR SPARE TIME TO TRAIN FOR AND FLY AT AIR DISPLAYS.

demonstrating remarkable skill in formation flying, the Blue Eagles also highlighted the genuine enthusiasm displayed by members of the Corps for their craft. The original Blue Eagles team consisted of five instructors from Middle Wallop who practised in their own time and used their own spare time to stage their displays. They proved to be such a hit at events during the summer of 1968 that their programme was much expanded for the following year and they became a full-time operation.

Flying light blue Sioux helicopters, by the mid-seventies the Blue Eagles were mounting displays all over the UK, as well as in Germany. Their routines became more complex and more entertaining each season, although no formal tuition in close-formation flying techniques was provided in the regular training routine for AAC pilots. Instead, the team's six pilots were drafted in from operational squadrons at home and abroad to undergo eight weeks' intensive instruction with the Blue Eagles. Then, throughout the spring and summer months, they were committed entirely to rehearsal and public displays. The Blue Eagles' Sioux may not have been as fast as the Folland Gnat advanced jet trainers in use by their RAF counterparts, the Red Arrows, but then the Red Arrows could neither spin on the spot nor fly backwards – not unless something had gone seriously wrong! Although the Corps would eventually decide that the cost of running a full-time display team was too heavy a burden, the team itself persisted, sustained by the spare-time enthusiasm of all those involved, under a variety of names that were to include the Army Eagles, Sparrowhawks and the Silver Eagles. Displays, too, were undertaken using team members' free time and they were to persevere for many years, maintaining the AAC's association with display flying in the hope that they might one day be given official status once more.

Far from the fun of the Blue Eagles summer displays, the situation that gave the gravest cause for British military concern as the sixties drew to a close was the growing unrest in Northern Ireland. Civil rights demonstrators clashed with the RUC in Derry in the summer of 1967, beginning a period of violent protest that was to lead to a cycle of terrorist atrocities, revenge and reprisal attacks from both sides of the sectarian and political divide. Army units stationed in the province, including the Queen's Dragoon Guards Air Squadron with its Sioux helicopters, were reinforced, the first time this had happened since the Second World War. Troops were deployed on the streets in support of the RUC during civil disturbances in 1969, with six Sioux of the 17th/21st Lancers Air Squadron operating from RAF Aldergrove to the north-west of Belfast.

As the military presence in the province increased, so too did their requirement for air support and by 1973 there were 15 Scouts, 23 Sioux and three Beavers in Ulster based at Aldergrove, Ballykelly, Omagh, Long Kesh and Sydenham. During the course of the next decade, AAC and RAF aircraft were also to turn a base at

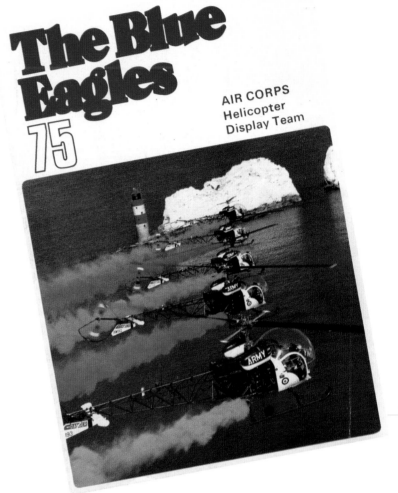

ABOVE: : BY THE TIME THIS 1975 PROGRAMME WAS ISSUED, THE BLUE EAGLES WERE TOURING ALL OVER BRITAIN DURING THE SUMMER DISPLAY SEASON AND WERE VENTURING FORTH INTO EUROPE.

Bessbrook Mill in the village of Bessbrook, in County Armagh, into Europe's busiest heliport. The former linen spinning mill was a major centre of operations for the security forces patrolling the border with the Irish republic. A flight would arrive or depart from Bessbrook every few minutes during the daytime with around 600 flights every week in and out of the base.

The tasks performed by aircrews throughout Northern Ireland were many, varied and often complex. They would fly recce sorties along the meandering border between Northern Ireland and Eire; search for suspect or hijacked vehicles on the roads; seek out suitable sites for observation posts; carry out surveillance on premises prior to raids by the security forces or carry out surveillance of suspected booby-trapped vehicles; observe and

TOP: NITESUN SEARCHLIGHTS LIT UP A TARGET AREA WITH EITHER A WIDE OR A PINPOINT BEAM, PRODUCING 3.5 MILLION CANDLE POWER.

ABOVE: A PA SYSTEM WITH A WOOFER OF WHICH ANY BOY RACER WOULD BE PROUD.

RIGHT: THE AAC PIONEERED THE USE OF PASSIVE NIGHT VISION GOGGLES IN NORTHERN IRELAND.

photograph marches, demonstrations, funerals or other public gatherings; seek out sniper locations in both rural and urban environments and, of course, assist in casualty evacuation of civilians as well as personnel of the security forces.

They also mounted 'Eagle Sorties', usually as a flight of two helicopters. A Sioux would carry a patrol leader, while a Scout transported his four-man detachment. The soldiers would sit back-to-back in the Scout with their legs outboard, their feet on the skids. This allowed for speedy disembarkation to set up a control point on a country road, search farm premises or investigate suspected bomb sites. In some places, such as border outposts, the only way to bring men and supplies in and out safely was by helicopter as slow-moving Army convoys were such tempting targets for roadside bombs. Any military vehicle, in fact, ran the risk of attack. Following the deaths of REME Sergeant D. Reid, Lance-Corporal D. Moon and Para Private C. Stevenson in June

ABOVE: A BEAVER OVER BELFAST, WHERE THE AIRCRAFT WAS USED FOR LIAISON AND VIP FLYING BUT ALSO PROVIDED INVALUABLE SERVICE AS A STABLE PLATFORM FOR RECONNAISSANCE AND SURVEILLANCE PHOTOGRAPHY.

1972 when their vehicle was blown up on their way to recover a downed helicopter, aircraft that had made forced landings off base were subsequently recovered by RAF support helicopters working with REME technicians.

Helicopters were also required to fly at night. Although ill-equipped to do so in the beginning, ingenious solutions were introduced to solve operational problems. 'Nitesun' searchlights of 3.5 million candlepower were fitted to Sioux for tasks such as lighting up landing sites for other helicopters or floodlighting civil disturbances. The Siouxs' 'Nitesuns' were also used for illuminating electricity pylons, the pilots patrolling miles of power lines at night to check the vulnerable pylons which were such an easy target for terrorist bombers.

By 1976, night flying in Northern Ireland was made more interesting by the initial introduction of night vision goggles which became a boon to pilots tasked with inserting covert patrols into sensitive border areas. Other AAC technical innovations in Northern Ireland included the 'Heli-Tele'. Helicopters and Beavers had been used for aerial photography of civil demonstrations, military installations and general surveillance purposes since the onset of

'the Troubles'. The stills taken were often supplemented by TV footage shot by an observer using a standard, hand-held camera, but 1976 saw the first deployment of the Heli-Tele, an airborne, real-time, data-linked television surveillance system that has since been adopted by police forces and security agencies around the world.

The use of airborne infra-red, false colour and other photographic equipment was also pioneered by the AAC in Ulster, with the REME helping to devise ever more ingenious pieces of kit. Infra-red searchlights, for example, were improvised by cunning REME technicians from Chieftain spotlights. In 2006, in recognition of the groundbreaking work carried out by everyone involved over almost four decades in Northern Ireland, 5 Regiment AAC was honoured by the Guild of Air Pilots and Air Navigators with the award of the Sir Barnes Wallis Medal for 'an exceptional contribution to aviation'.

By the mid-seventies there were more than 100 REME staff in Northern Ireland keeping the AAC airborne. Interestingly, they found that the helicopters in the province, putting in more flying time than they did anywhere else, suffered fewer niggling problems – a case of everything working better when it is in regular use.

WESTLAND GAZELLE AH MARK 1

SPECIFICATION

→ Engines	1 x Turbomeca Astazou III N2 592 shp
→ Maximum Level Flight Speed	193 mph
→ Cruising Speed	164 mph
→ Service Ceiling	16,405 feet (5000 m)
→ Range	310 miles
→ Armament	None normally fitted
→ Overall Length	39 feet 3 inches (11.97 m)
→ Height	10 feet 5 inches (3.18 m)
→ Main Rotor Span	34 feet 6 inches (10.5 m)
→ Maximum All-Up Weight	3,968 lb (1800 kg)
→ Payload	1,000 lb (454 kg)
→ Crew	1 pilot plus 1 crewman and up to three passengers

'THE GREAT THING ABOUT THE GAZELLE IS THAT IT IS AN UNCOMPLICATED BEAST, DOES WHAT IT DOES VERY WELL AND IS CHEAP TO RUN'.
LIEUTENANT-COLONEL STEVE HIMBURY, COMMANDING OFFICER 7 REGIMENT AAC

The Gazelle was originally conceived to fulfil a Frency Army requirement for a light utility helicopter, then, along with Puma and Lynx, became part of the Anglo-French, three-aircraft, development agreement of the late 1960s. Although the Gazelles destined for the AAC were built by Westland, the aircraft was designed by Aérospatiale and bore a strong family resemblance to its predecessor, the Alouette. The Gazelle, however, represented a significant advance over the old Alouette, using composite materials in its rotor blades and a special 13-blade enclosed tail rotor called a fenestron that achieved dramatic reductions in noise levels. Although the early aircraft suffered from disturbing vibration problems, these were resolved by the time the Gazelle entered service with the AAC in 1973. In fact, four different versions of the aircraft served with all four branches of the British Forces – Army, Navy, Marines and RAF. During its amazing thirty-five years of service with the AAC, the Gazelle has operated in environments as diverse as the deserts of Iraq and the antarctic conditions of the Falklands. Like many helicopters, it suffers a slight reduction in performance in hot and humid conditions but has otherwise proved itself to be a thoroughly reliable workhorse, becoming a great favourite with its air and ground crews who have dubbed it the whistling chicken leg.

1967 – 1977

ABOVE: DURING EXERCISE HORN BEAK IN THE FRENCH PYRENEES IN 1974, 653 SQUADRON SERGEANT-MAJOR HAROLD DE-ST-CROIX MAKES CONTACT WITH THE FRENCH MOUNTAIN FLYING SCHOOL AT SAILLAGOUSE.

ABOVE: THE FLAG IS UNFURLED AT THE SUMMIT OF MONT BLANC IN THE FRENCH ALPS AFTER A SUCCESSFUL ASCENT BY AN AAC TEAM IN 1975.

Regular use, of course, meant heavy servicing schedules. A Sioux could easily average four times as many hours under the spanner as it did in the air and even the more modern Gazelle, with which the Sioux was gradually replaced from 1974 onwards, required a short morning's check-over every 25 hours as well as an 800-hour service that took three weeks.

There was no shortage of work for the REME staff in the province, especially when aircraft returned to base peppered with bullet holes. Terrorist gunmen fully realised the importance of the AAC to the security forces in Northern Ireland and never missed an opportunity to try to make a name for themselves by bringing down an Army aircraft. In the main, the noise and vibration in their helicopters meant that aircrews were blissfully unaware when they came under fire, only realising that they had been hit when the bullet holes were later pointed out to them by their ground crews. In 1974, a warning device was developed to help pilots take evasive action when they were being shot at and it was

tested by the first Director of the AAC, Major-General Roy Dixon, who endured a few tense moments '. . . flying in a Scout fitted with such a device up and down a small arms range between the firing point and the butts while a marksman fired rifle shots beneath us. I was not entirely confident and expected at any moment to feel a searing pain somewhere in my anatomy . . .'

Just as the ongoing process of reorganisation demonstrated the flexibility and adaptability of the AAC, so too did the myriad roles they undertook in Northern Ireland. Whether delivering vital supplies to farmers cut off by appalling winter weather, plucking stranded cattle from beaches cut off by the tide, or dropping an SAS patrol on a remote hillside at dead of night, the AAC continued to show that it was equal to any task it might be called upon to perform.

'I spent nine years in Northern Ireland, which was great experience,' says Bill Wright. 'The great thing about the AAC is that we understand what the soldiers on the ground want from us

'I WAS NOT ENTIRELY CONFIDENT AND EXPECTED AT ANY MOMENT TO FEEL A SEARING PAIN SOMWHERE IN MY ANATOMY'

ABOVE: A SCOUT OVER HONG KONG, WHERE THE AAC SUPPORTED TROOPS ON THE GROUND PATROLLING THE BORDER WITH CHINA.

RIGHT: AN AIR GUNNER'S VIEW OF THE COUNTRYSIDE WHILE ON PATROL.

and so we offer a good level of support. Northern Ireland enabled us to use our aircraft and equipment to best advantage.'

Northern Ireland may have been the AAC's busiest operational environment, but their biggest commitment of manpower and machinery continued to be in Germany. Patrolling the border with East Germany, standing ready and training to respond to any incursion by the WP into West Germany, the AAC operated out of a dozen different facilities. Detmold was the main AAC base with a workshop, although the HQ AAC 1 (BR) Corps was at Bielefeld.

Most soldiers who have been involved in 'live' wars agree that combat consists of a short period of intense, adrenalin-fuelled action during a firefight, bracketed by long periods of routine training and monotonous inactivity. Although the tension during particularly 'warm' periods of the cold war was very real, the confrontation never actually erupted into open combat, so the training continued and, while never entirely inactive, the soldiers of the AAC devised countless ways to fight off the monotony.

Corporal David 'Hank' Hancock well remembers one of the ways that ground crews killed time when their aircraft disappeared off into the German countryside. 'As a technician, waiting around in the early hours of the morning for aircraft to return could be a bit boring. Thank goodness for uckers! Looking back, it was amazing how seriously we took that game. It might have been

based on Ludo, but it was much more tactical than that. It's played with two dice, instead of one, and has 'blobs', where a player has two or more pieces on the same square which forms a barrier to block an opponent's movement. But a major part of the game is about cheating and not getting caught!

Uckers competition there at the Blue Beret Club, which was the name of the 9 Regt Attic Bar. It was between the senior ranks, who were dressed as gentry, against the junior ranks, dressed as peasants. It was fiercely competitive because pride was at stake.

'It's strange because the game was such a big deal within the context but, once I left the AAC, it meant nothing. People find it hard to understand why we were so passionate about Uckers.'

Just like personnel in every other British Army unit, those who served in the AAC enjoyed the range of competitive sports that were supported and organised by the Army. Hank Hancock didn't spend all of his free time hunched over an uckers board.

'I also threw myself into sport,' he recalls. 'I boxed for the AAC and was captain of the boxing team in Northern Ireland for two

109

1967 – 1977

ABOVE: UCKERS AT DETMOLD IN THE BLUE BERET CLUB WITH THE TOFFS AGAINST THE PEASANTS.

LEFT: CORPORAL 'HANK' HANCOCK (RIGHT) IN ACTION FOR THE AIR CORPS AS A WELTERWEIGHT.

years running. I had eight fights and never lost a bout. I was light middle and then welter weight. I also played rugby.'

Keeping fit in the Army was always to be encouraged, especially when there were so many other temptations on offer. 'We used to complain about the food,' says Hancock, reflecting the favourite gripe of soldiers throughout history, 'but, looking back, it was excellent. We could eat as much as we wanted – everything from fish and chips to a full roast. Nobody ever went hungry.

'And there was a bar in the cellar of the 71 Workshop in Detmold, called The Keller. A lot of weekends would be spent there. There was a happy hour every Friday when all the ranks would get together. Cigarettes and alcohol were tax-free and so they were much cheaper than they would be in the UK.'

Such comforts were not always available to AAC personnel stationed at the British Army's largest training area. BAOR in Germany may have hosted the greatest concentration of AAC personnel and equipment, but BATUS in Canada is an area so vast that it can swallow up all of the German training zones with room to spare for Salisbury Plain and the rest of the UK training facilities, too. The tract of Alberta prairie covers an area of 2690 km^2 (slightly larger than Luxembourg) to the northeast of Suffield and is a Canadian Forces Base, although it is BATUS (British Army Training Unit Suffield) which makes most use of the countryside. Since 1972, 29 Flight have formed the AAC's permanent presence at Suffield. Initially, this consisted of just two Sioux and a Beaver.

ABOVE: A GAZELLE SHADOWS A SOVIET MIL MI-8 'HIP' WHILE PATROLLING THE BORDER IN GERMANY.

111

1967 – 1977

Their job was primarily to be on call for casevac during training exercises, transporting casualties as far as the hospital in Medicine Hat to the south east of the training ground, but BATUS AAC Flight also worked closely with the civil authorities in the area, fire spotting, rescuing adventurous walkers or canoeists and even once transporting an unusual underslung load – the excavated skeleton of a dinosaur.

The Beaver also served as VIP transport and was ideally suited to the rugged terrain of the Canadian prairies. Since its introduction in 1961, the Beaver had provided sterling service in Aden, Borneo and the Far East where it received high praise for its reliability. Having originated in Canada, first flying in 1947, the Beaver was, of course, equally suited to the far-from-tropical environment of the harsh Canadian winters. The Beaver would go on to fulfil its role as a liaison and photo reconnaissance aircraft until its gradual replacement by the Islander, the last BATUS Beaver departing the base in 1985, although that aircraft is still believed to be working hard today in Canada's Northern Provinces.

The Sioux based at BATUS were eventually retired in 1977, heading, like so many other North American retirees, to Florida. They were not to enjoy a complete retirement in the sun, however, as they had been bought by the police department in Miami. The Sioux were replaced by the more modern Gazelle, which had actually entered service with 660 Squadron at Soest some three years earlier. Developed by Aérospatiale in conjunction with Westland, the Gazelle bore a family resemblance to the Allouette, with which it also shared the distinction of having record-breaking performance. In 1971 it flew at an average speed of 296 km per hour over a closed circuit of 100 km and demonstrated a top speed of around 310 km per hour (193 mph). Although the MOD initially intended to order 569 Gazelles for the Army to replace the Sioux and extend the capacity of the light observation helicopter fleet, this number was subsequently cut to 212 with nine of those machines allocated to the Royal Marine Commando Helicopter Squadron, which trained with the AAC at Middle Wallop.

The Gazelle entered service on schedule and became one of the few Army helicopters to do so without the kind of teething problems that had marred the introduction of so many of its predecessors. The same could not be said of its future stablemate, the Lynx. Originally intended to replace the Scout at the same time as the Gazelle took over from the Sioux, the Lynx was dogged by development problems. Its spectacular performance, however, was to make its delayed introduction well worth the wait.

CHAPTER SIX

BACK IN THE FIRING LINE
1977 – 1987

In late 1977, the AAC finally began taking delivery of the long-awaited Lynx utility helicopter. The Lynx had been developed as part of a co-operational effort between the British and French governments aimed at fulfilling their armed forces' requirements for three different helicopter types. An outline agreement signed in 1965 followed by a more detailed plan in 1967 identified the areas of responsibility for the development of the three aircraft. One was to be a tactical supply and support helicopter, which would become the Puma; the second was to be a light observation helicopter, which would become the Gazelle; and the third was a utility, reconnaissance and anti-tank helicopter. This was to become the Lynx.

The first two of the three aircraft in the programme were to be designed by Aérospatiale in France and the third was the responsibility of Westland in the UK. Although Westland had already embarked on design studies for a twin-engined machine that would fit the bill, the French were much further ahead with their projects. The Puma prototype had actually first flown in 1965 while the first Gazelle prototype took to the air in 1967. The Lynx, designed to meet the requirements set out in the British Army's 'General Staff Operational Requirement 3335' of October 1964 for a medium-sized, multi-role helicopter to enter service in 1972, did not actually get off the ground until February 1971.

The delays had been caused mainly by engine development problems. There had been no engine available when the Lynx was being designed that would provide enough power to give the required speed and lift capabilities. Problems with excessive vibration from the rotors, overheating and poor power delivery persisted throughout the Lynx prototypes' flight trials. Despite these worries, in June 1972 the first development aircraft in Army utility configuration gave a tantalising glimpse of what was to come when it set a new world speed record for its class, achieving 321.74 km per hour (199.92 mph).

One of the main reasons why 1972 had originally been chosen as the in-service date for the Lynx was because it was envisaged that by that time at least part of the Scout fleet would be coming to the end of its operational life, with metal fatigue making it increasingly

LEFT: TROOPS WERE CRAMMED INTO THE PROTOTYPE LYNX DURING THE SEVENTIES TO TEST DIFFERENT SEATING CONFIGURATIONS.

ABOVE: DESPITE THE TECHNICAL DIFFICULTIES, THE EARLY LYNX DISPLAYED ENORMOUS PROMISE DURING FLIGHT TRIALS.

difficult to maintain airworthiness. In fact, the Scouts had to soldier on far longer, although many did begin to show their age. Extensive exercises were undertaken during the mid-seventies to evaluate the 'airmobile' infantry concept. It might be assumed that the British Army was simply following on after their American counterparts in developing techniques for using aircraft to put troops on the ground exactly where they were required, the Americans having used helicopters to such good effect in this respect in Korea and Vietnam, but it should be remembered that the British had been deploying airborne troops by parachute and glider since the Second World War. The capabilities of modern helicopters simply allowed them to begin experimenting in fulfilling yesterday's aspirations with today's technology. The technology of today, however, did not always hang together quite as well as might have been expected. AAC and RAF helicopters worked in close cooperation to explore the benefits of infantry detachments becoming airmobile. Armed with Milan anti-tank missiles, squads were dropped in strategic

locations during exercises designed to thwart the movements of enemy armour. The speed with which they could be deployed in West Germany added another dimension to the strategy for countering a Warsaw Pact advance.

The potential problems faced by the British Army's helicopter fleet in fulfilling this role began to reveal themselves when the stalwart Scouts started to show their age. Although described in 2008 by Staff Quartermaster Lieutenant Colonel Colin Chick as his favourite helicopter because it was 'a soldier's aircraft' that was 'infinitely repairable', the mobility trials in the seventies often taxed the Scouts to the extent that their reliability was called into question.

Clearly, the new Lynx could not be brought into service quickly enough, although not all of the bugs had been ironed out by the time the AAC took delivery of its first Mk 1 aircraft. The main shortcoming was a lack of power, despite the fact that, in 1986, a modified Lynx set an as-yet-unbeaten world speed record for

ABOVE: THE SOLDIERS WHO WERE USED AS GUINEA PIGS FOR THE LYNX'S CASEVAC TRIALS HAD IT NO BETTER THAN THOSE WHO DID THE SEATING TESTS.

helicopters of 400.87 km per hour (249.09 mph). The Mk 1 Lynx would ultimately undergo retrofitting to improve its performance but, in the meantime, the first 100 aircraft (an initial Army order of over 160 was subsequently slashed in the 1974 Defence Review) began to demonstrate their versatility in Germany with 651 Squadron at Hildesheim and 654 Squadron at Detmold.

Although capable of carrying up to nine passengers, the Lynx was intended for use not only as a tactical troop transport, but also to replace the Scout as a tank buster. Armed with eight TOW (Tube-launched, Optically-tracked, Wire-guided) missiles mounted four either side of the fuselage, the Lynx could carry a further eight missiles as reloads inside the cabin. The gunner sat in the port seat and used a roof-mounted gyro-stabilised sighting system. Maintaining the target in his sights kept the missile on track up to a range of 3,750m, a distance it could cover in just 21 seconds. While this represented a significant improvement over the Scout's capability, it wasn't until 1981 that the Lynx was ready for service with TOW. Until then, it was used in its utility role.

In October 1979, the first Lynx were deployed in Northern Ireland. Flt Lt P Luker AFC, an RAF exchange pilot who would go on to attain the rank of Air Vice Marshal with the JHC, was involved in the introduction of the Lynx to BAOR and served as a flight commander with 654 Squadron when they began a four-month 'Operation Banner' tour in Northern Ireland. In Luker's subsequent report giving his impression of the impact that the Lynx had in the province, he made it clear that he understood that there were some misgivings about the deployment of the new aircraft, delays in its introduction having led some to refer unkindly to it as the 'Egyptian-built, Anglo-French designed Sphinx'. The flight of six aircraft (plus one reserve Lynx) operated mainly out of the Armagh and St Angelo bases, the five pilots and five crewmen, supplemented by the Squadron Commander and 2IC taking a pilot's slot, providing a twenty-four hour capability, the night aircraft being fitted with Nitesun lights.

LEFT AND BELOW: FUN WITH A SERIOUS MESSAGE – THIS BOOK OF CARTOONS WAS DESIGNED TO INTRODUCE SOLDIERS TO THE NEW LYNX.

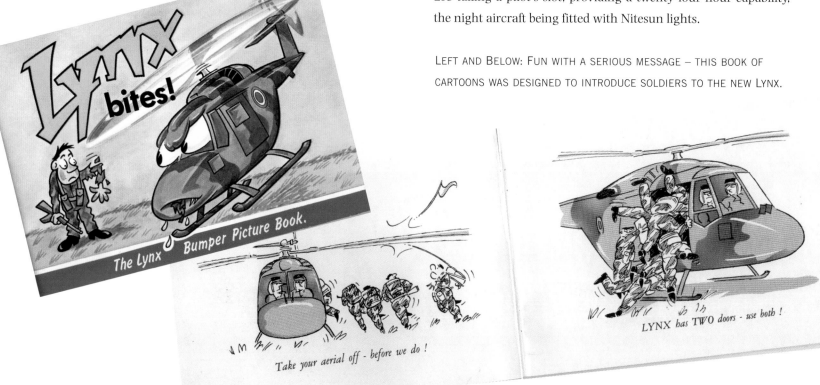

ABOVE: THE LYNX, SEEN HERE OVERFLYING THE NORTHERN IRELAND PARLIAMENT BUILDINGS AT STORMONT, WAS DEPLOYED ON ITS FIRST TOUR IN THE PROVINCE IN 1979.

Although the Lynx crews were called upon to perform all manner of tasks, ninety per cent of their role was in troop insertion and extraction, a job that often had to be carried out with great speed. The Lynx quickly showed its form, Luker noting that, '. . . it only needed two or three practical demonstrations to show that we could be airborne within five minutes of receiving the first call-out, by day or night.' The Lynx's avionics also allowed it to fly in the kind of weather that would have grounded lesser machines. As Luker pointed out, 'All those who fly in Northern Ireland in winter will know only too well how frequent, localised patches of bad weather can hamper operations . . .' The Lynx was able to cope with the worst of Ulster's weather, the Decca Tactical Air Navigation System (TANS) in particular giving the aircraft a much-improved night-time, poor weather and low-visibility capability. During that first winter deployment, the Lynx achieved ninety-eight per cent availability, only once failing to provide twenty-four-hour cover from one of their bases. This was a dramatic improvement over other types and stands as a tribute to the air and ground crews operating the Lynx, although they struggled nonetheless to cope with the bane of every helicopter's existence – the squaddie.

'The cabin of the Lynx is small at the best of times,' Luker reported, 'but shrinks dramatically when filled with eight wet, muddy, cold, tired Marines equipped with Bergens, radios, weapons, webbing and waterproofs; attempting to supervise the cabin from the front of the aircraft when picking up eight of the same from an OP, two hundred yards from the border at night, is next to impossible.

BRITTEN-NORMAN ISLANDER AL MK 1

'IT WAS A LITTLE UNNERVING TO BE REMINDED THAT A SINGLE SPECIALIST CAMERA, SIMILAR TO THAT FITTED TO THE SPACE SHUTTLE, WAS MORE VALUABLE THAN ALL THE ISLANDERS IN THE UNIT ...'

LIEUTENANT-COLONEL BILL WRIGHT EX OC 1 FLIGHT

Britten-Norman is an independent aircraft manufacturer based at Bembridge on the Isle of Wight. Their BN-2 Islander began life in 1963 as a design for a civil light utility, cargo and passenger aircraft. The original prototype flew in 1965 and by April 1967 the first production model was airborne. It was to become the best-selling commercial aircraft produced in Western Europe.

Seven Islanders joined the AAC fleet in 1989, flying with 1 Flight from Aldergrove in Northern Ireland to replace their ageing Beavers and with the Advanced Fixed Wing Aircraft flight at Middle Wallop. In its operational role, the Islander is used for photographic reconnaissance and intelligence gathering, liaison flying, the carriage of senior officers and the delivery of important spares or equipment. As well as providing a reconnaissance and surveillance service, the Corps' Islanders have also worked with the Police conducting missing persons searches, with the Ordnance Survey and with the Customs and Excise service.

In 2003, four of the slightly larger Defender models were ordered with more advanced surveillance equipment, under-wing drop tanks to extend the aircraft's range and defensive aids dispensers to counter the threat of ground attack.

SPECIFICATION

→ Engines	2 x Allison 250 turbo props
→ Maximum Speed	225 mph
→ Cruising Speed	178 mph
→ Service Ceiling	13,600 feet (4,145 m)
→ Range	437 miles
→ Armament	None
→ Overall Length	35 feet 10 inches (10.93 m)
→ Height	13 feet 9 inches (4.2 m)
→ Wingspan	49 feet (14.93 m)
→ Maximum Take-off Weight	7,000 lb (3,630 kg)
→ Crew	1 pilot plus up to 6 passengers

ABOVE: LYNX EQUIPPED WITH TELEVISION SURVEILLANCE EQUIPMENT FOR USE IN NORTHERN IRELAND.

'Consequently, doors get left open, handles are forced off, headsets jettisoned, fire extinguishers dropped, windows released and boot-prints found on the cabin roof . . . the aircraft itself does not help in that it is still not soldier-proof – the emergency jettison handle is positioned as an invitation to tired troops to rest their boots on it, the door mounting is too flimsy and the door handle designed so that unfamiliar and confused hands attempt to rip doors off the aircraft . . .'

It could be argued, of course, that the only way to 'soldier-proof' any vehicle, let alone a helicopter, is never to allow soldiers in it in the first place! But it wasn't only tired and muddy patrols against whom the Corps' helicopters needed to be protected in Northern Ireland.

In their excellent book *Army Aviation in Ulster*, authors Guy Walker and Alex Boyd reproduced the testimony of a tactfully anonymous Royal Military Policewoman who had attended a

dawn raid on a house during which a suspect was apprehended. On being informed that she was to return to base by helicopter, she strode towards the waiting Scout only to find the rear cabin occupied by two burly RUC officers with the prisoner sandwiched between them. It was clear that she was expected to take a seat up front alongside the pilot, although she quickly realised that her uniform skirt would restrict her movements to such an extent that some careful manoeuvres would be required to preserve any semblance of dignity.

For some reason, she seemed to think that kneeling on the floor of the cockpit would be the best way to start climbing aboard, but wobbled a bit and started to overbalance as she did so. 'With lightning instinct I grabbed for a handhold,' she recalled. 'Unfortunately, I grabbed the collective pitch lever and the helicopter took off.' Naturally, this took everyone on board somewhat by surprise, not least the pilot, to the extent that the RMP

ABOVE: THE LYNX DID NOT IMMEDIATELY REPLACE THE SCOUT IN ALL OF ITS ROLES, THE SCOUT SOLDIERING ON, ESPECIALLY IN SUPPORT OF SPECIAL FORCES.

and one of the RUC officers promptly fell out. The pilot quickly recovered control of his machine, bringing it back down to earth, whereupon the RMP picked herself up off the ground and clambered aboard, any attempt at a dignified embarkation now abandoned. She then spotted the RUC officer banging on the door on the pilot's side. 'He was alternately knocking and pointing downwards in what appeared to be a mixture of pain, annoyance and shock,' said the RMP. 'This seemed to me a silly attitude; he had not fallen from a great height – well, not a very great height . . .' What she didn't immediately realise was that the pilot had landed with one skid on the unfortunate RUC man's foot.

The end of the seventies also saw the completion of the most recent round of AAC reorganisation, including the formation of

Northern Ireland Regiment AAC in November 1979. This did not bring an end to the rotation of squadrons from Germany for service in Ulster, but the permanent presence of 655 Squadron and the establishment of a formal command and administrative structure allowed for greater efficiency in day-to-day operations. The nine Scouts and six Gazelles of 655 Squadron were joined by a fixed wing flight of Beavers, later Islanders, from 7 Regiment as well as a second squadron rotating from Germany every four months. Once the Lynx units in Germany became more specialised in the anti-tank role, however, the time spent stripping them down and re-equipping them at the beginning and end of each tour became so prohibitively inefficient that in 1986 665 Squadron was reformed as part of Northern Ireland Regiment, equipped

'THE AIRCRAFT. . . IS NOT YET SOLDIER-PROOF — THE EMERGENCY JETTISON HANDLE IS POSITIONED AS AN INVITATION TO TIRED TROOPS TO REST THEIR BOOTS ON IT . . .'

ABOVE: A 656 SQUADRON GAZELLE OVER SALISBURY IN RHODESIA ON OPERATION AGILA PEACE MONITORING DUTIES DURING WHICH THE SQUADRON ADOPTED THE 'PANGOLIN AIRWAYS' SHOULDER FLASH (BELOW LEFT).

with Lynx and Gazelle. To maintain the required manning levels, personnel were drafted in from Germany for tours in the province with the squadron. Originally created as a Canadian AOP unit during the Second World War, the squadron title had been 'retired' in 1945, revived in 1969 to fly Scout and Sioux and lost again in 1978 during reorganisation. In 1987, the squadron adopted a new badge which incorporated the Canadian maple leaf and an Irish harp to represent its 'international' history.

The end of the seventies also saw the AAC take on a new peace-keeping role when 656 Squadron, having been recalled from their traditional home in the Far East and all but disbanded in 1977, was reformed at Farnborough and despatched to Rhodesia on Operation Agila. The former British protectorate of Northern Rhodesia had become independent and been renamed Zambia in 1964 after which Southern Rhodesia had declared itself independent of the UK and renamed itself simply 'Rhodesia'. A protracted civil war ensued with the minority white population determined to cling to power despite being outnumbered by their black countrymen 22:1. When a shaky peace deal was finally brokered in 1979, a Commonwealth Monitoring Group (CMG) was established to oversee open and fair elections in the territory. The guerrilla groups agreed to gather at sixteen Assembly Points (APs) where they were monitored by CMG detachments, just as the government forces were also kept under watch.

The guerrilla fighters, battle-hardened by years of brutal bush combat, were distrustful of the CMG detachments and the Scouts and Gazelles of 656 Squadron. Working in coordination with RAF C-130s and Pumas, 656 Squadron made regular supply and mail runs to the different APs, beginning operations on Christmas Day 1979, the Scouts flying out of a base at Gwelo and the Gazelles from Salisbury. Major S. R. Nathan, 656 Squadron Commander, remarked that the guerrillas '. . . were never entirely relaxed when we were in the air. At all locations they covered our approach with at least one AA machine-gun and, whilst the aircraft were on the ground, with small arms and RPG 7 . . . in the first few days we gave away hundreds of cigarettes . . . and showed them round the helicopters in order to create some kind of trust. What else can you do when armed with only a 9 mm . . . ?'

The entire three-month deployment was incredibly stressful for all of those involved, including the REME and RAOC support units, with over 2,200 flying hours accumulated, but the general

BELOW: A ROCKET-EQUIPPED GAZELLE DURING OPERATION CORPORATE ON THE FALKLANDS ISLANDS.

ceasefire held throughout the election period. The Squadron returned to the UK knowing that Operation Agila was a job well done, the deputy commander of the CMG, Brigadier John Learmont adding his congratulations in a letter stating that; 'In the early days you and your pilots were literally the lifeline for the soldiers at the rendezvous . . . it was a magnificent performance and it will never be forgotten by those you supported . . .'

There was to be little time, however, for 656 Squadron to rest and settle into normal training patterns. On 2 April 1982, Argentina invaded the Falklands Islands. The Falklands are a self-governing Overseas Territory of the United Kingdom but had been claimed as sovereign territory by Argentina ever since Britain took possession in 1833. The dispute over the islands manifested itself from time to time in sabre-rattling manoeuvres by the Argentine navy but they had never previously gone so far as to stage a full-scale invasion. When just such an operation was mounted in 1982, the small detachment of Royal Marines on the islands mounted a valiant defence against the invaders but, in the face of overwhelming odds, were ordered to surrender on 4 April. British Prime Minister Margaret Thatcher vowed that the islands would be reclaimed, by force if necessary, and even as diplomatic

ABOVE: A FALKLANDS GAZELLE SHOWING ITS HARRIER-DERIVED MATRA ROCKET SYSTEM AND WITH A ROYAL NAVY WESSEX IN CLOSE COMPANY.

pressure was brought to bear on Argentina, a joint task force set sail for the South Atlantic.

The Royal Navy's aircraft carriers HMS *Invincible* and HMS *Hermes* were accompanied by a plethora of support vessels, eight destroyers, fifteen frigates, six submarines and over forty vessels taken up from the Merchant Navy strung out along the 8,000-mile route. When diplomatic measures failed to dislodge the Argentines, 'Operation Corporate', the British invasion to retake the islands, was authorised.

The Royal Marines Air Squadron and elements of 656 Squadron AAC were embarked with the task force and, along with the Sea King, Wessex and Lynx of the Royal Navy, were to fly vital sorties in support of the troops on the ground. The first elements of the task force had set sail just three days after the Argentine invasion but preparations for others were to take a few days longer.

The AAC and the Marines were to send a total of 12 Scouts and 15 Gazelles into action. The Scouts were armed with SS11 missiles and specially-fitted machine guns but it was decided that the normally unarmed Gazelles needed to be able to pack a punch, too. The French MATRA SNEB 68 mm rocket system, as fitted to the RAF's Harriers, was deemed an effective self-defence weapon, although neither a detailed specification for fitting nor official clearance for use with the Gazelle existed. An AAC Beaver was flown to France to pick up a set of rocket pods and ammunition, the pods then being fixed to outriggers on a Gazelle by Westland engineers. A special sight was adapted and fitted, with firing trials conducted on Easter Monday. A contract for supply of the weapon was signed with MATRA and REME engineers began making modifications for fitment of the rockets on 17 April, just ten days after the idea for arming the helicopters was first muted.

ABOVE: THE NATURE OF THE FALKLANDS TERRAIN MEANT THAT THE USE OF LAND VEHICLES WAS NOT FEASIBLE, TROOPS RELYING HEAVILY ON THE SCOUT AND GAZELLE FOR RESUPPLY.

The task force, meanwhile, had to face up to the threat from more than 100 enemy fighter aircraft based on the Argentine mainland while assembling an invasion force to tackle the 10,000 troops occupying the Falklands. The Argentines had also deployed around 20 Pucara ground-attack aircraft on the islands. The work of the AAC and Royal Marine helicopters began when the main amphibious assault went in on 21 May. The Marines deployed nine Gazelles and six Scouts during the landings with an advance element of four Scouts from 656 Squadron also initially falling under their command. Although the main landings at San Carlos Water went largely unopposed, a Royal Marines Gazelle flying in support of a Sea King to the north was hit by small-arms fire. Although mortally wounded, the pilot, Sergeant A.P. Evans managed to ditch in the sea and his crewman, Sergeant E.R.

Candlish, dragged his dying friend ashore. Within minutes, another RM Gazelle was also hit and crashed, killing both the pilot, Lieutenant K. Francis and his crewman Lance-Corporal B. Griffin. A third RM Gazelle was also damaged by enemy fire but made it to the safety of a landing ship.

When the *Atlantic Conveyor* supply ship fell prey to an Argentine Super Étendard jet on 25 May, suffering strikes from two Exocet missiles, six Wessex and four Chinook helicopters it had been transporting were lost. This served to multiply the demands placed upon the Scouts and Gazelles. Their size and manoeuvrability allowed them to operate in areas where larger machines would have presented too large a target and, with the terrain in the Falklands precluding the use of vehicles for the resupply of forward units, the RM and AAC units operated round

the clock. Although poorly equipped for night operations and largely unfamiliar with the night vision goggles used by the RM crews, the AAC aircraft utilised their limited payloads to the full, flying ammunition and stores in and lifting casualties out. While the pilots dodged enemy fire, the aircrewmen tended the wounded as best they could, saving many lives in the process.

It was not only ground fire with which the helicopter crews had to cope. Argentine aircraft conducted regular sorties over the island, the supply and transport ships at anchor providing

tempting targets for their bombs and missiles, although they would also engage other targets of opportunity before heading for home on the mainland. The AAC scouts supporting the Paras on the high ground above the landing areas could not afford to be caught napping by an Argentine raider. On 27 and 28 May, 2 Para headed south for Goose Green with RM aircraft in support. Two of the RM Scouts fell foul of Argentine Pucaras. One of the Scout pilots, Lieutenant R.J. Nunn was killed and his crewman, Sergeant A.R. Belcher, seriously wounded, although he survived the crash. Captain J.G. Greenhalgh and Sergeant R.J. Walker of 656 Squadron took over from the two RM Scouts. They continued to ferry in supplies and evacuate casualties in the teeth of intense Argentine small arms and artillery fire during a battle that raged for fourteen hours. Captain Greenhalgh's determined efforts to recover serious casualties leading to his award of the DFC.

The remainder of 656 Squadron arrived in the Falklands towards the end of May, closely followed by 70 Aircraft Workshops and 1 Aircraft (Stores) Support Unit. Working in far from ideal

conditions, fighting foul weather and pervasive ground water as well as fending off Argentine attacks, the REME and RAOC personnel nevertheless managed to maintain a daily aircraft availability in excess of ninety per cent. And every aircraft counted as the infantry pressed on at pace. AAC Scouts spearheaded a heliborne assault on Swan Inlet while SS11 missiles were unleashed on an Argentine patrol at Egg Harbour House where the helicopters were inserting Observation Post (OP) parties from 1/7 Gurkha Rifles. Eight Argentines armed with anti-aircraft missiles were captured.

In order to take the islands' capital, Port Stanley, the surrounding high ground had to be secured. The Gurkha and Scots Guards' assaults on Mount William and Tumbledown mountain were supported by 656 Squadron. The helicopters transported OP detachments, ferried combat supplies from their base at Fitzroy Settlement and evacuated casualties to hospital ships. For his courage in flying repeatedly into the thick of the battle to recover seriously wounded soldiers from the slopes of Tumbledown mountain on 14 June, Captain S.M. Drenman was awarded the DFC.

The Argentine defence all but collapsed on 14 June, the infantry advancing rapidly to engage any enemy positions with any fight left in them and AAC Scouts seeking out gun emplacements, bunkers and other strongholds to target with their SS11s. Later that day, the Argentines surrendered.

As in all such conflagrations, there had been tragedies in the heat of battle. An AAC Gazelle piloted by Staff Sergeant C.A. Griffin with Lance-Corporal S.J. Cockton as his crewman was ferrying a Royal Signals party to a problematic radio rebroadcast station at night when they were mistaken for an enemy aircraft and shot down. There were no survivors aboard the Gazelle. One Scout narrowly avoided being hit by a British Blowpipe missile and several aircraft dodged

RIGHT: THE FALKLANDS VICTORY AS CELEBRATED IN THE ISLAND'S MAGAZINE, THE PENGUIN NEWS.

incoming 'friendly' small-arms fire. Flying at night or in poor visibility at low level over a battlefield, it is almost inevitable that such cases of mistaken identity will occur.

Even once the fighting was over, there was still a great deal of work at hand for 656 Squadron's aircraft. They established a base of operations at Port Stanley and flew in support of infantry patrols, mine clearance parties and Rapier Air Defence batteries as well as helping to return some of the Falkland Islanders to their isolated farms.

The spoils of war from the Falklands campaign included two Agusta A109 helicopters. The twin-engined, eight-seat utility machines proved to be such an attractive proposition that two more were ordered to replace the Scouts of 8 Flight which were based at Stirling Lines, providing special operations support for the

30th JUNE 1982   No. 20

THE PENGUIN NEWS

THE FALKLAND ISLANDS NEWS MAGAZINE

VICTORY

The date : MONDAY, 14th JUNE 1982

The place : NOT "Puerto Rivero", "Puerto de las Islas Malvinas" OR "Puerto Argentino" BUT PORT STANLEY, FALKLAND ISLANDS

The event : Surrender of all Argentine forces in the Islands

FREEDOM

AND A

FUTURE

The following message reached Prime Minister Thatcher in the early hours of Tuesday, 15th June 1982 –

" H.Q. Land Forces Falkland Islands, Port Stanley.

In Port Stanley at 9 o'clock pm Falkland Islands time tonight 14th June 1982, Major General Menendez surrendered to me all the Argentine Armed Forces in East and West Falkland, together with their impediments.

Arrangements are in hand to assemble the men for return to Argentina, to gather their arms and equipment, and to make safe their munitions.

The Falkland Islands are once again under the government desired by their inhabitants. God save the Queen. "

(Signed) J. J. Moore.

69 Sqn AAC
ast day Falklands
June 1985

Our 747
Mt Pleasant Airfield

FI VIP
ENCLOSURE

ABOVE: THE FALKLANDS SQUADRON WAS FORMED BY 656 SQUADRON IN 1982, BUT OTHERS WERE TO FOLLOW THEM SOUTH OVER THE YEARS.

SAS at Hereford.

The unofficial celebrations marking the end of the Falklands campaign had barely died down when the party spirit drifted on into the celebrations to mark the twenty-fifth anniversary of the AAC. An air show was organised at Middle Wallop, which drew an enormous crowd of members of the public but also served as a reunion for over 2,000 members of the AOP, GPR, REME, RAOC, pilots and ground crews who were proud to have served with the Corps over the years. The occasion also served to establish a new memorial and book of remembrance dedicated to all of those who had lost their lives in the service of Army flying.

The historical theme continued during the year when the Museum of Army Flying was relocated to purpose-built premises at the edge of Middle Wallop. The foundation stone for the new building was laid by Sandhurst graduate and helicopter pilot King Hussein of Jordan.

WESTLAND LYNX
AH MK 7/9

The most advanced helicopter of the AAC's fleet when it was introduced, the Lynx was a more complicated machine than those previously flown by Army pilots and, although user-friendly up to a point, it could be a very demanding aircraft. The rewards when pilot and aircraft worked in harmony, however, were outstanding. The performance of the Lynx was remarkable. It set, and still holds, the world speed record for helicopters, clocking up 249.09 mph (400.87 km per hour) and has proved its agility not least in the hands of the AAC helicopter display team, the Blue Eagles, who perform barrel rolls, loops and back flips with the Lynx. They spend almost as much time flying it upside down as they do with the aircraft the right way up.

From the time that it first entered service in 1977, the Lynx has undergone almost continuous development. The engines were gradually upgraded, giving the AH 9 a significant payload advantage over the original aircraft, while its tricycle undercarriage replaced the skids, prompting some to nickname it 'the wheelie bin'. One of the most significant improvements in the gradual upgrading of the AH 1 to AH 7 standard (prior to the introduction of the AH 9) was the redesign of the tail rotor. It was made larger and turned in the opposite direction, improving performance by eliminating an element of interference that had existed between the tail rotor and the down-draught from the main rotor.

Although the TOW missile system with which the Lynx was equipped is now redundant, the aircraft's anti-armour role having been taken over by the Apache, the Lynx will continue to serve in the utility role for which it was originally conceived until the introduction of the 'Future Lynx' Battlefield Reconnaissance Helicopter in 2013.

SPECIFICATION

→ Engines	2 x Rolls-Royce Gem turboshafts
→ Maximum Level Flight Speed	205 mph
→ Cruising Speed	144 mph
→ Range	550 miles
→ Combat Radiius	62 miles approx with 2-hour loiter
→ Armament	8 x TOW Anti-tank missiles
→ Fuselage Length	39 feet 7 inches (12.06 m)
→ Height	11 feet 2 inches (3.4 m)
→ Main Rotor Span	42 feet (12.8 m)
→ Maximum All-Up Weight	10,500 lb (4,763 kg)
→ Crew	2 pilots, or 1 pilot plus 1 crewman, and up to ten passengers

While the Lynx was still being settled in to its anti-armour role, proposals were being considered for the next generation of attack helicopters. The Lynx was, of course, a utility machine, initially designed for tactical troop insertion and resupply. The benefits of being able to deploy a dedicated attack helicopter had been apparent since the Americans developed their Huey 'gunships' in Vietnam and they had been operating the specialised Cobra since 1967. Its slim fuselage made it less of a target on the battlefield while its speed and firepower made it a formidable weapons platform. Its replacement was already on the drawing board and

got on with their job. Although trained to land the aircraft in an emergency, the weapons specialists were under the command of the pilot. When compared with the traditional set-up in, for example, a tank, the old helicopter command system started to look completely unbalanced. A tank commander does not do the driving. Instead, he instructs the driver, so that the tank can be manoeuvred into the best possible position either for the deployment of its weapons or its own self defence. This line of thinking led to the 'CREST' crew restructuring scheme where the specialised Lynx attack machines adopted a second pilot. The

the Russians were about to introduce the Mil Mi-28 'Havoc' attack helicopter, developed as a slimmed-down version of the Mi-24 'Hind' gunship. The concept of the attack helicopter was clearly moving on and the future role of the AAC in its offensive capacity now needed careful consideration.

In the meantime, the manner in which the Lynx and its crews were being trained was quickly evolving. The traditional arrangement had always been that the pilot was in command of the helicopter, flying the aircraft while the gunners or observers

ABOVE: MAJOR BLOUNT, FORMER OC 663 SQUADRON, TESTS HIS DESIGN FOR A NEW ATTACK HELICOPTER.

senior member of the crew was in command of the aircraft and its weapons systems while the pilot concentrated on flying. When operating under nuclear, biological and chemical warfare conditions, or at night, or in bad weather, the two pilot system helped to spread the cockpit workload.

Naturally, this opened up even more opportunities for those

'. . . I BECAME A PILOT BECAUSE I WAS SICK OF OTHER PILOTS TRYING TO KILL ME'

ABOVE: GROUND CREWS HAD TO TRAIN HARD TO ACQUIRE EVER MORE COMPLEX SKILL SETS THROUGHOUT THE EIGHTIES, HANDLING THE LYNX'S TOW SYSTEM BEING JUST ONE OF THEM.

aspiring to be pilots and it became commonplace for a corporal to be found in the right-hand pilot's seat. Getting there, however, involved a more fraught period of training for some than it did for others. Stefan Galek became a pilot because he thought it was the best way of keeping himself alive. 'I became a pilot because I was sick of other pilots trying to kill me!' he admitted. 'I started off in the infantry and when I was in Northern Ireland I saw a Scout

helicopter arrive with supplies and I thought that it looked exciting. So I approached my platoon commander about applying for aircrew and he replied, "Don't be ridiculous, Galek, you can't even drive a Land-Rover."

'But I became an aircrewman, then an airgunner and, after three crashes, through no fault of my own, I decided that if I was going to die then I will do it myself. So I took a pilot's course in 1983 and, unbelievably, it was on that course that I had my fourth crash. I was learning instrument flying and they smeared the screen of the cockpit white so that I couldn't see out. But the instructor started showing me the circuit pattern, because that

ABOVE: FAR FROM BEING CONSIGNED TO THE SCRAPHEAP BY THE ARRIVAL OF THE LYNX, SCOUTS SUCH AS THIS ONE WITH 7 FLIGHT IN BRUNEI WOULD CONTINUE IN SERVICE INTO THE NINETIES.

BELOW: PERSONNEL FROM 7 FLIGHT ENJOYING A REFRESHING SPOT OF JUNGLE SURVIVAL TRAINING IN BRUNEI.

was what we were due to do next, and he lost concentration as we were coming in to land. The wing of the aircraft caught the control caravan and it landed on its side and came to a halt upside down. We must have been doing 70-80 knots.

'The emergency services were on the scene quickly and I was dragged out to the smell of leaking fuel. The instructor was fine but I had broken my back and was put in traction for a month to sort it out. Two months later I went back to the flying course.

'Of the previous crashes I was involved in, the most bizarre was when we had to pick up a general and his entourage. It was a hot day when we took off in the Scout and at about four hundred feet there was an almighty bang. The engine died, we smashed into the deck and the Scout went belly up. The General said to the pilot, "Are we actually going to get this aircraft going or are we just going to bugger about?"

'We later discovered that the cause of the crash was the General's flak jacket. He had taken it off because of the heat and

his adjutant had hung it up on a bolt on the exterior of the helicopter. When we moved forward it was sucked into the engine. We took the rap for that, not the General or his adjutant, because, ultimately, it was our responsibility.'

While pilots like WO1 Galek practised their skills on the training grounds in Germany, as the eighties drew to a close war clouds were gathering on the horizon once again.

With his country's economy devastated by a protracted war with Iran, Iraqi leader Saddam Hussein turned with envious eyes towards the prosperous neighbouring state of Kuwait. Allies in the war against Iran, Kuwait had funded Iraq's campaign to the tune of billions of dollars, the war debt becoming the rock on which their uneasy relationship was about to founder.

BELOW: BY THE END OF THE EIGHTIES, LYNX AIR AND GROUND CREWS WERE WELL TRAINED AND FULLY PREPARED FOR WHATEVER MIGHT COME THEIR WAY.

CHAPTER SEVEN

THE DESERT AND OTHER
STORMS   1987 – 1997

As the deteriorating relations between Iraq and Kuwait created an increasingly tense atmosphere in the Gulf, the world looked on, few willing to believe that, after eight years' of war with Iran, Saddam Hussein would lead his people into another conflict. With one of the world's largest armies at his disposal, however, any threats issued by Hussein had to be taken seriously.

In the meantime, rather than the desert sands of the Iraq/Kuwait border, some in the Army Air Corps had their eyes fixed on the stars. In November 1989, Major Tim Mace was selected, along with scientist Helen Sharman, to join Project Juno, a private British scheme working in partnership with the Soviets to conduct a series of experiments in outer space. Over 13,000 aspiring British astronauts applied to join the training programme. Major Mace, with a degree in aeronautical engineering, was ultimately to be Helen Sharman's 'back-up' on the project, training as an astronaut – or cosmonaut as the Russian version is known – ready to step in should anything happen to prevent Sharman from making the trip. Helen Sharman did, of course, make it into space, the Soyuz TM-12 rocket delivering her to the Mir space station in May 1991. Tim Mace did not get the chance to fly in space, although he did marry the daughter of a former Russian cosmonaut, but had he flown in Sharman's place, would he have been able to lay claim to being the first AAC officer to do so? Some

would say not . . . The personnel of 666 (V) Squadron AAC, which operates in support of 7 Regiment AAC (V), have some justification in saying that one of their pilots was the first AAC man in space, albeit that he was an AOP pilot. The squadron was formed in March 1945 at RAF Andover as an RCAF unit, manned by Canadian air force personnel and AOP-trained Canadian artillery officers. One of those officers was James Montgomery Doohan. He had joined the Royal Canadian Artillery at the outbreak of the Second World War, aged just nineteen, receiving a commission as a lieutenant in the 13th Field Regiment. Posted to the UK in 1940, he then spent four years in training before taking part in the D-Day landings, going ashore at Juno Beach – coincidentally the same name as Tim Mace's space programme. Doohan led by example during the fighting, reportedly taking care of two German snipers personally, but came to grief in the darkness on the first night on French soil when he was checking his own sentries. One nervous young squaddie fired at the figure in the dark and Doohan was hit by six rounds from a Bren gun. While recovering from his wounds back in the UK, he decided to learn to fly, becoming an AOP pilot.

What has this to do with outer space? The connection comes over twenty years later when Doohan, having long since left the Army and embarked on a career as an actor, starred as 'Scotty' the Chief Engineer aboard the USS *Enterprise* in the original *Star Trek* television series. If you don't think that counts as actually having flown in space, then Doohan still has the last laugh. In accordance with one of his last requests, following his death in 2005, Doohan's ashes were blasted into space aboard a rocket.

LEFT: MAJOR TIM MACE TRAINED WITH THE SOVIETS AS A COSMONAUT, HAVING BEEN SELECTED FROM 13,000 APPLICANTS TO TAKE PART IN PROJECT JUNO.

ABOVE: THE ISLANDER ENTERED SERVICE WITH 1 FLIGHT IN NORTHERN IRELAND IN 1989, ULTIMATELY TAKING OVER FROM THE TRUSTY OLD BEAVERS.

Flying a little closer to the ground in 1989, the Beaver Flight, part of 5 Regiment based at RAF Aldergrove, changed its name to 1 Flight in anticipation of the arrival of the DHC Beaver's replacement, the Islander. Many were sad to see the Beaver Flight go, its aircraft having become a familiar sight in the skies over Ulster during the past twenty years, but the final pair left Aldergrove in June 1989, the first of 1 Flight's five Islanders having arrived three months earlier.

The Britten-Norman Islander began life as a design concept in the early 1960s when John Britten and Desmond Norman decided to expand their business from the manufacture of crop-spraying equipment to the production of aircraft. Of the three aircraft they initially proposed to build, the BN-2 Islander was by far and away the most successful. The twin-engined, utility and cargo aircraft made its first flight in 1965 and went on to become one of the most successful civil aircraft ever produced in Britain. By the time the Corps took delivery of its Islanders, the aircraft was a tried-and-

tested design and had benefited from improvements to its aerodynamics as well as uprated, three-bladed, turbo-prop engines. Its STOL (Short Take-Off and Landing) capability meant that it could take off from a runway under 385 yards (350 m) long and it was rugged enough to utilise rough strips, grass runways or beaches. The aircraft was reasonably quiet and had the endurance to be able to stay in the air over a target area for lengthy periods, making it ideal for use over urban areas where it could remain on station without causing too much disturbance.

The Islander's main role, of course, was to be aerial reconnaissance and photography, its cargo bay giving it the ability to carry as much camera equipment for high-level, low-level or oblique photography as might be required, plus a range of electronic surveillance equipment. The aircraft has proved to be both efficient and economic to fly and maintain as well as being thoroughly reliable, providing civil assistance to various authorities including a number of police forces tracking down

1987 – 1997

ABOVE: THE FOUR GAZELLES AND THE LYNX OF THE BLUE EAGLES FLYING IN FORMATION WITH FIVE ALOUETTE III AIRCRAFT OF THE DUTCH 'GRASSHOPPERS' DISPLAY TEAM.

missing persons and customs officers searching for drugs smugglers or people traffickers. An AAC Islander even helped out when survey photographs of London's Heathrow Airport were required, making scores of low-level passes without ever causing any disruption to the airport's busy flight schedules.

The Islander is also used for communications and liaison duties. Although the civil 'airliner' version of the Islander can accommodate up to ten passengers, the AAC machines, not configured

entirely as transport aircraft, can generally take only six, plus the pilot and co-pilot or crewman. It was for use primarily as a communications aircraft that one of 1 Flight's Islanders was deployed to Saudi Arabia in 1991 in preparation for Operation Granby.

Saddam Hussein's negotiations with Kuwait had gone from bad to worse until he eventually accused the Kuwaitis of stealing

LEFT: A 'FREE KUWAIT' STICKER SPORTING THE RED-AND-GREEN COLOURS OF 4 REGIMENT.

Iraq's oil by 'slant-drilling' to access oil deposits on the Iraqi side of an oil field that straddled the border between the two countries. He demanded compensation, clearly angling to cancel out his debts to Kuwait, and amassed an army of 100,000 men along the border. This was viewed by most as sabre-rattling on Saddam's part. Such border confrontations had happened before, not least because Iraq had in the past attempted to claim the state of Kuwait as a southern territory of Iraq. British paras and marines had been deployed along the Kuwait/Iraq border in 1961 under a defence treaty when one of Saddam's predecessors had made moves to annex Kuwait. Having convinced Western diplomats that his troop deployments were, in fact, just a show of force, Saddam then shocked the international community with his audacity by sending his tanks and helicopter gunships across the border into Kuwait in the early hours of 2 August 1990.

ABOVE LEFT: MAJOR STUART SLADE, FORMERLY THE AAC CO IN KUWAIT, WENT TO THE GULF WITH 4 REGIMENT ON OPERATION GRANBY TO CONDUCT THEATRE FAMILIARIZATION TRAINING.

TOP RIGHT: WHILE SOME GAZELLES RECEIVED DESERT COLOURS FOR OPERATION GRANBY, OTHERS SPORTED UN LIVERY IN CYPRUS.

ABOVE RIGHT: FLYING WAS CLEARLY FAR SAFER THAN TRAVELLING BY ROAD IN CYPRUS!

Saddam's invasion and his troops' brutal treatment of the Kuwaiti people was condemned by the United Nations, who issued demands for him to withdraw. Preparations were put in hand to send military units from a coalition of different countries, led by the United States but including a number of Arab nations, to Saudi

BELL 212 HP AH MK 1

'THE BELL 212 IS A DREAM TO FLY, EXTREMELY
RELIABLE AND HUGELY CAPABLE . . .'

LT COL BILL WRIGHT, BEAVER PILOT AND LEADER OF THE AAC HISTORIC AIRCRAFT FLIGHT

The Bell 212 aircraft serves with 7 Flight in Brunei and 25 Flight in Belize where its exceptional 'hot and humid' operating characteristics, coupled with its load lifting capacity and winch, make it the ideal aircraft for missions in such difficult terrain. Derived from the Bell 205 UH-1, known as the 'Huey' after its original designation of HU-1 (Helicopter, Utility) when first evaluated by the U.S. military in the late fifties, the 212 bears a close family resemblance to its predecessor. It does, however, have two engines as opposed to the 205's single engine and is sometimes referred to as the 'Twin Huey'.

The 212 retains the two-blade rotor configuration of the old Huey and can carry an impressive complement of fully-laden troops or an underslung load of up to 2,500kg. The load capabilities of the Bell 212 proved invaluable when 7 Flight's aircraft left Brunei to assist in relief operations following the Boxing Day Tsunami in 2004.

SPECIFICATION

→ Engines	2 x Pratt & Whitney PT6T - 3B TwinPac turboshafts, 1800 shp
→ Maximum Level Flight Speed	150 mph
→ Cruise Speed	115 mph
→ Service ceiling	17,400 feet (5,300 m)
→ Specialist equipment	Winch Underslung bucket for firefighting
→ Range	288 miles
→ Armament	None
→ Total length	57 feet 3 inches (17.46 m)
→ Fuselage length	42 feet 5 inches (12.92 m)
→ Height	14 feet 5 inches (4.39 m)
→ Main Rotor Span	48 feet 2 inches (14.69 m)
→ Empty Weight	5,511 lb (2,500 kg)
→ Maximum Weight	11,023 lb (5,000 kg)
→ Crew	2 plus 13 passengers

Arabia to protect the Saudi border from the threat of further Iraqi expansionism.

The British contribution included an armoured division with 4 Regiment AAC as the Divisional Aviation Regiment. The regiment began moving out of its bases in Germany in early December 1990 with twenty-three Lynx, twenty-four Gazelles, the RHQ and squadrons as well as the workshops and support units all heading for the Persian Gulf in a logistical operation that became multi-national in its own right. Lindsay Rumgay was a WO2 with 659 Squadron, unloading transport aircraft as they arrived at Al Jubayl in Saudi Arabia on the Persian Gulf coast. 'USAF C5 Galaxies arrived with six Lynx and two Gazelles,' he recalled. 'The first one took seven hours to unload and a lot of jiggery-pokery! We were better prepared for the second C5, and that took two hours to unload.

'The rest of 4 Regiment's helicopters arrived on heavy lift Belfasts . . . They carried two Lynx and one Gazelle or a variation of kit towards the end. The section became expert unloaders, and took forty-five minutes to disembowel the Belfast.'

The Regiment remained in Al Jubayl for four weeks, carrying out environment training before deploying into the desert. The only proper road, the desert tracks aside, was the pipeline road that ran north-west into Iraq. This, like every other supply route, was now handling far more traffic on both the 'up' and 'down' carriageways than it had ever been designed to take, and the traffic that was far wider, to boot. There were regular near-misses, and many 'fender benders' as Corporal Spike Wright discovered when travelling in a 659 Squadron LAD 4-tonne truck.

BELOW: EQUIPMENT AT AL JUBAYL PRIOR TO MOVING OUT TO THE DESERT CAMPS.

ABOVE: TENTED ACCOMMODATION WAS FAR FROM COMFORTABLE, ESPECIALLY WHEN TRUCK DRIVERS DEMOLISHED THEM DURING THE NIGHT.

'The drivers had just changed,' he recalled, 'Corporal Mayfield taking over from Sergeant Duffy. The long haul began again – the game of "chicken" with the tank transporters resumed. Unfortunately, after five minutes, the score was US Tank Transporters 1, 659 LAD 4-Tonners 0, when a tank transporter over-stepped his mark and strayed slightly onto our side of the road.

'In a split second we'd lost half the side of the 4-tonner, one side of a trailer and a complete trailer wheel, and very nearly ninety per cent of the LAD. Pulling over to the side of the road, the damage was assessed as repairable. Wheels were changed and mud guards ripped off, the REME "variable adjustment tool" coming in very handy.'

Anyone who had been looking forward to a spot of mid-winter desert sunshine was in for a disappointment. There were very few of the scorching hot days that might have been expected in that part of the world. Instead, there was an almost constant wind, driving sand and grit everywhere, temperatures that dropped well below freezing at night and enough rain to make anyone think that they were actually back home in the UK. The tented accommodation, strung out along the roads and tracks among the sandbagged defences, supply dumps and vehicle parks was far from comfortable, especially when truck drivers, moving without lights, strayed a little off line, demolishing guy ropes to bring the tents crashing down.

During a formation exercise prior to the coalition advance into Iraq, driving without lights or GPS, Corporal Mick Green came to know the frustration of driving over open desert terrain. 'Corporal Parkinson in his Rover had hit a trench and the trailer had turned

ABOVE: THE LYNX WAS TO PROVE ITSELF AS AN ANTI-ARMOUR ATTACK HELICOPTER IN THE DESERTS OF THE PERSIAN GULF.

upside down, so we stopped and gave him a hand with the recovery . . . He drove off for about fifteen metres and drove straight into another trench, so we had to go and recover him again.'

By the time they got moving, their convoy had left them far behind, but catching up with the tail lights was no easy task. 'All we could see were these little red lights in the distance, and we didn't know which lights were our convoy,' Green recalled. 'We were on radio silence, so we couldn't call up and ask them. So we thought that we would flash our lights. But lights responded from every other convoy out in the desert. No one knew which one was ours.'

Corporal Green's experiences, which included having to recover a Sultan which almost disappeared into a trench system, were far from unusual, but provided valuable experience in traversing the desert for all concerned. The potential dangers the regiment faced prior to actually going to war were of a kind much closer to home. Lance-Corporal 'T' Tithecott remembered one hazard that his section faced on a daily basis – their water boiler. 'Nobody liked lighting it . . . the SQMS was saved from charred hands by his gloves . . . ask Captain King about the sudden loss of both his eyebrows and most of his fringe. Constantly during the day there were explosions coming from the cookhouse, provoking comments like, "I wonder who the boiler got this time?"

'Remarkably, everyone came home fit and well after facing the boiler and the Iraqis for four months – but then we still had to contend with the boiler!'

Training continued, as did the round-the-clock work of 71

'. . . ASK CAPTAIN KING ABOUT THE SUDDEN LOSS OF BOTH HIS EYEBROWS
AND MOST OF HIS FRINGE . . .'

ABOVE: TRACKED UNITS FOUND THE GOING FAR EASIER THAN WHEELED VEHICLES WHEN THE RAIN SOFTENED THE DESERT SURFACE.

LEFT: A VOUCHER THAT COULD BE EXCHANGED FOR A LITTLE EXTRA 'COURAGE'.

VOUCHER

THANKS FROM COURAGE

As a tribute to the men and women of our armed forces in the Gulf, COURAGE, the forces' favourite brewer, in association with **The Sun** and will exchange this voucher for a drink of FOSTER'S LAGER or JOHN SMITH'S BITTER at any NAAFI bar.*

*One Voucher per person
*Expiry date 31 December 1991.

Aircraft Workshop, fitting sand filters, GPS, Radar Warning Receivers and all manner of modifications. Aircrew had to keep themselves up to speed with a welter of information generated by the Americans' command-and-control systems, including SPINS (weekly Special Instructions), ACOs (Air Control Orders), IFF (Indicator: Friend or Foe) transponder codes, authentication codes and airspace control frequencies, as well as the regiment's own divisional briefing data and extra information should they need to operate inside US Marine Corps air space. Collating all of this in their personal information packs added forty minutes to their preparations before taking to the air, as much of the information changed on a daily basis.

On 17 January 1991, while 4 Regiment was still in Al Jubayl, eight American Apache AH-64 and two Pave Low helicopters opened the air war against Iraq during an operation to take out radar sites near the Iraqi/Saudi Arabian border. The air campaign that followed saw any Iraqi aircraft flying against the allies shot down and the rest of their air force either destroyed on the ground or fleeing to Iran. Bombing raids and missile attacks on strategic targets continued until Sunday 24 February, when the American 7 Corps launched their ground attack into Iraq, the French 6th Light Armoured Division on their left flank while the British 1st Armoured Division pushed forward on the right.

Major-General Rupert Smith, in command of the 1st Armoured Division, chose to deploy his helicopters along with his artillery to form the 'Depth' fire group responsible for striking targets behind the enemy's front lines. Attacks by Lynx, with TOW missiles, on enemy armour could then be best co-ordinated with artillery bombardments, Gazelles having a target acquisition and AOP role to play in any case. It was not the AAC helicopters that pressed home the advance in the first instance, however, but the

AAC soldiers on the ground. Captain Mark Terry was with the foremost of 654 Squadron's vehicles as they joined the Battle Group on 23 February. '654 Squadron moved up to the Queen's Royal Irish Hussars Battle Group assemble area, the tracks some one and a half hours ahead of the wheels, the wheel element now including some 58 vehicles of 2/6 Cav's FARP as they didn't have any form of navigation equipment whatsoever.'

The tracked vehicles made reasonable progress over the unforgiving terrain, through rain-softened desert sands, towards the staging area where they were to spend the night. 'The wheels had a different story,' admitted Captain Terry, 'their route being littered with bogged down and broken down vehicles. Progress was similar to that on a motorway blocked with road-works on a glorious bank holiday . . . very slow!'

The REME and FARP units showed formidable perseverance, however, and were ready to move out again the next morning. 'I

BELOW: IRAQI PRISONERS SURRENDERING UNDER THE WATCHFUL EYE OF A LURKING LYNX.

ABOVE: EXCAVATING THE REMAINS OF A WRECKED IRAQI HELICOPTER WAS HOT WORK WHEN THE WEATHER FINALLY IMPROVED.

could see the Squadron's huge wheeled convoy about one to two kilometres off to the east,' Captain Terry recalled. 'One enemy aircraft would have had a field day. Fortunately they were sensible and stayed at home. We crossed into Iraq at 1307 hours, four minutes ahead of the wheeled convoy.'

The next day, the regiment's aircraft flew forward to join the ground units at their forming-up point behind the QRIH and between an artillery battery and an MLRS battery with its 227 mm rockets. As Captain Terry put it, 'Noisy people, gunners.' The weather, however, continued to be appalling, cold and wet with wind speeds of 50 knots. Corporal Rex Butt of HQ Squadron was making his way from the forward positions back to regimental headquarters in the gathering gloom of the early evening when

his driver spotted several figures coming towards them across the desert. 'As I looked across,' Corporal Butt later reported, 'it seemed that one of them was waving a white flag. Behind the five men we saw what we thought was a berm.'

Having tried in vain to reach regimental headquarters by radio to request instructions, Corporal Butt decided to investigate further, quickly discovering that what they thought was a berm, or defensive earthwork, was nothing of the sort. 'Me and the driver dismounted, leaving our radio operator trying to get through to RHQ. We then went over to the Iraqis and made them kneel down with their hands up.

'They could only speak a little English, but we managed to talk to one of them who pointed to an officer. We went up to him and asked how many there were, where they were going and all the rest of it. He said that about two hundred men wanted to surrender. When we looked again into the distance, we saw that there was no berm at all, but a big bunch of people standing together. We started to feel a bit apprehensive as we had been hearing reports that prisoners had up and fired at people . . .'

Despite the fact that their instructions from RHQ were to let the surrendering prisoners go, Corporal Butt and his two companions pressed their superiors to allow them to guard the prisoners until a more suitable detachment could be despatched as they quickly learned from the officer that he had many sick men. The Iraqis were also clearly terrified when any aircraft flew over, having been on the receiving end of the allied air bombardment. The three men formed the prisoners up into lines and watched over

LEFT: THE WORKLOAD IN KUWAIT WAS HECTIC, BUT THERE WERE STILL MOMENTS TO RELAX IN THE SUN.

them until the RSM arrived. 'We set up machine guns and had guarded the Iraqis for another four or five hours when the Coldstream Guards turned up,' Corporal Butt remembered. 'Luckily we had been issued with brown biscuits the day before, so we were able to give the prisoners one biscuit each. Their officer was upset because apparently there was no biscuit left for him.'

Bad weather continued the next morning (26 February) but by mid-day it cleared just in time for three Lynx and three Gazelles of 654 Squadron to embark on armed reconnaissance patrols in support of a QRIH attack. Their job was to follow up an artillery barrage to check if the way ahead was clear of enemy armour and, if not, to clear it. The patrols did not take long to find targets. While

Captain Avery, an American on secondment to the AAC, along with Staff Sergeant Isherwood in their Lynx engaged an enemy tank on the northern flank, Captain Chris Morley and Staff Sergeant Seymour, working with the squadron commander, Major Eustace, identified more Iraqi armour in the shape of MT-LB personnel carriers.

'We had the OC with us at this stage [in a Gazelle] and once he confirmed the targets as hostile, we engaged them,' reported Captain Morley. 'We moved forward behind the tanks of the QRIH at 15-20 knots and engaged more targets. When they were destroyed we moved to the northern flank where we engaged two T-55s alongside [Gazelle pilot] Sergeant Thompson's armed recce patrol.'

Avery and Morley's first shots on the T-55 tanks were forced off target by excessive turbulence due to the rapidly deteriorating weather conditions. Further rounds, however, were successfully tracked onto their targets to devastating effect. 'The weather deteriorated and we weren't able to continue,' recalled Captain Morley. 'So we aborted the mission and returned, via the CP, to the Squadron location. In all we destroyed four T-55s and three MT-LBs.'

The following day, Lieutenant Chris Nagle was airborne with a patrol of two Lynx and two Gazelles, clearing an area forward of the advance towards Kuwait City. 'Towards the end of our patrol we discovered, to the north of our position, several vehicles apparently abandoned. In accordance with orders given the night before to destroy anything that appeared to be serviceable, we attacked the position with TOW missiles fired from the two Lynx, assisted by two other Lynx which had joined the patrol. A total of fourteen missiles were fired at the position. After scoring one- hundred-per-cent-perfect hits, we made the wry discovery that it was a decoy position made of wood and other materials. It had done its work well – but it was good to get the chance at last to fire some missiles!'

The following morning 659 Squadron was tasked with supporting an advance by the 7th Armoured Brigade. Staff

ABOVE AND RIGHT: SURVIVAL TRAINING BACK HOME. YOUR OWN
BIVOUAC IS NEVER AS INVITING AS THE ONE THE INSTRUCTOR BUILT.

Sergeant 'Jeep' Smith was in command of a TOW-armed Lynx.
'After a while I heard the OC calling the fire team forward. The
visibility was between five hundred metres and one kilometre in a
smoky haze. Luckily, with the thermal imaging sight, I could see
right through it . . . By this time, a few targets were visible, but were
obviously abandoned. I then observed a moving target slowly going
right to left about five kilometres distant. I identified it as hostile, but
smaller than a tank. I decided to engage.

'The vehicle stopped and one person got out and ran away. I fired
and the missile struck dead centre. Shortly afterwards we flew past
the burned-out hulk of a Gaz 69 jeep with a black scorch mark on the
back. We carried on. The OC said, "No one is to fire unless I say so." I
bleated back that I had just engaged a jeep . . . the ceasefire was
minutes away and the battle group was now on Weapons Hold.'

Staff Sergeant Smith fired one of the final shots of what some

were to call 'The 100 Hours War', although 4 Regiment's work
was not yet done. No sooner was the ceasefire declared than the
first fair weather of the campaign set in and with it came a
maelstrom of taskings for the helicopters. They flew through the
inferno of the oil well fires and, although they became well
established in their base some forty miles west of Kuwait City, they
were to return to Germany before long. Lieutenant-Colonel (later
Colonel) Mike Wawn was truly impressed with the AAC
performance during the entire operation. 'I was CO of 4 Regiment
during Operation Granby in Kuwait. We went out in December
1990 and returned just before Easter 1991 and I was very proud
of my men and the job we did there. We were involved in

ABOVE: A GAZELLE DEPARTING A BORDER OUTPOST IN NORTHERN IRELAND. SUCH INSTALLATIONS COULD ONLY BE RESUPPLIED BY AIR.

intelligence gathering, reconnaissance, armed action against enemy armour, casualty evacuation, moving equipment and material about the place – pretty much everything, really.

'One of the things that sticks in my mind is the adaptability of the British soldier. We dragged him out of his snow-covered base in Detmold, Germany, dressed him in camouflage, painted the vehicles a sandy colour and within days we were operating in an entirely different environment in which different rules apply. But within about four weeks I was quite content that the regiment was one unit, working well together.

'Everyone had to get acclimatised very quickly and there's a lot of preparation required for helicopters to operate in a desert environment – new filters and all that sort of stuff. The grease on moving parts needs to be constantly cleaned and re-applied because when sand gets into it the mix becomes an abrasive paste. So it was a great challenge coping with that.

'The sand got everywhere – in your food and drink, in toothpaste and between you and the loo roll. That is a very uncomfortable experience, I can tell you!'

Operation Granby, including its '100 Hours War', had been an invaluable experience for the AAC. For the first time, the Lynx and Gazelle teams had been deployed on operations, in a combat capacity that was close to the 'tank-busting' role for which they had trained. The ground crews and logistical support teams proved that they could operate under adverse circumstances, including the ever-present threat of aerial bombardment with chemical weapons from Iraq's SCUD missiles, and still provide the service that was expected of them. Many lessons were learned along the way, lessons that would be carried forward into future conflicts.

ABOVE: THE NEW 5 REGIMENT WAS GIVEN PERMISSION TO ADOPT THE MOTTO OF THE OLD GLIDER PILOT REGIMENT, 'NOTHING IS IMPOSSIBLE'.

RIGHT ABOVE AND BELOW: A 'FAREWELL PARTY' WAS HELD FOR THE SCOUT AT MIDDLE WALLOP IN 1994 WHERE PILOTS OLD AND YOUNG PAID THEIR RESPECTS.

As 4 Regiment returned from the Gulf in 1991, the Northern Ireland Regiment, which had been operating from Ballykelly and Aldergrove, was centralised at Aldergrove as a prelude to further reorganisation within the constantly-evolving structure of the modern Army Air Corps. Northern Ireland was still a hotbed of activity, as witnessed in September 1993 when two Lynx escorting a Puma into Crossmaglen came under fire from multiple automatic weapons including two heavy machine guns mounted on the back of trucks. One of the Lynx gave chase as the vehicles sped off, the door gunner returning fire once he was sure he could do so without endangering nearby houses. Two further Lynx were quickly on the scene and the vehicles were cornered in a farm complex where the Provisional IRA gunmen made their escape. Several weapons and hundreds of rounds of ammunition were captured. A less fortunate Lynx was hit by two mortar rounds at Crossmaglen a few months

ABOVE: THERE'S ALWAYS TIME FOR SPORT, AS WITNESSED BY THESE SHOTS FROM THE AAC'S 1996 RUGY 7'S TOURNAMENT.

later, losing its tail boom. The aircraft was completely wrecked, although the crew managed to escape, the Air Door Gunner gaining a Mention In Despatches for his bravery in rescuing an injured RUC constable from the blazing aircraft.

The Northern Ireland Regiment became 5 Regiment AAC in 1993, joining the Corps' complement of 1 Regiment, then based at Hildesheim; 2 Regiment, comprising the training squadrons at Middle Wallop; 3 Regiment at Wattisham; 4 Regiment at Detmold and 9 Regiment at Dishforth. The squadrons and the few remaining independent flights were being reorganised to accommodate changing roles with new equipment. The Lynx AH 7 was in service as was the upgraded AH 9, easily identifiable with its wheels rather than skids. The new helicopters finally allowed a faithful old friend to slip into retirement. The last of the AAC Scouts was finally pensioned off (apart from the one flying with the Historic Aircraft Flight) in 1994. With almost forty years service in the Army, one of the many who look back on the Scout with great affection is Staff Quartermaster Lieutenant-Colonel Colin Chick.

'I love the Scout,' said Lieutenant Colonel Chick. 'The Scout is a great aircraft. It's a soldiers' aircraft. You can hit it with a hammer. You can kick it. You can bend it. It will go anywhere. It chops trees down without worrying about them. It's a good old bread-and-butter aircraft with simple technology that does the job. I am very fond of the Scout as is anybody from my era.'

As an aircrewman, Chick flew countless missions in the Scout in Ulster. 'The Scout did a marvellous job in Northern Ireland,

although not everyone was as keen on the aircraft as we were. I remember we had to take an Army dog handler and a search dog on board and the dog was not at all happy about getting into the helicopter. Most of the dogs used to be quite happy about getting into the aircraft but this one wasn't – and neither was his handler. Anyway, we got them both in and about halfway through the flight the dog became quite irate and decided to throw up all over the pilot. This then made the handler sick, too, and the whole inside of the aircraft was covered in puke.

'It was about two o'clock in the morning and we had to take them where they were going and then wait for about three hours to take them all the way home again. It didn't matter how hard we scrubbed it out, the aircraft stank of puke for about a week after that.

'We flew some strange missions in the Scout. I remember dropping off one SAS patrol very close to the Irish border. Four of them were dropped off but when we went back six hours later to pick them up there were six of them. And they were carrying a very strange bag. No one was quite sure what was in it, but it was very definitely body-sized and nobody mentioned it throughout the whole flight . . .'

As the Scout made way for newer equipment, 5 Regiment was experimenting with the sort of equipment that Army flyers had begun using more than a century before. Aldergrove played host for a while to a Westinghouse Skyship 500. The airship was flown

'. . . ABOUT HALFWAY THROUGH THE FLIGHT THE DOG BECAME QUITE IRATE AND DECIDED TO THROW UP ALL OVER THE PILOT . . .'

ABOVE: AAC PILOTS HAD THE CHANCE TO TRY THEIR HAND WITH THE WESTINGHOUSE SKYSHIP 500 WHEN IT UNDERWENT TRIALS WITH 5 REGIMENT IN 1995.

by AAC pilots in a series of trials but, while it could carry a useful payload and loiter over a target area for lengthy periods as a surveillance or reconnaissance machine, its limited speed, slow-moving vulnerability (it makes a big target) and limited capability in high winds meant that the Army was not about to return to ballooning just yet.

Mounting political tension in Yugoslavia drew the world's attention in the early nineties when friction between the six countries that made up the Yugoslav republic on the Balkan Peninsula – Bosnia-Herzegovina, Croatia, Macedonia, Montenegro, Serbia, and Slovenia – erupted into war. Croatia and Slovenia declared independence in 1991, with Bosnia-Herzegovina following suit a few months later. Territorial claims and ethnic differences prompted fierce fighting and appalling atrocities. The United Nations stepped in a year later, sending the United Nations Protection Force (UNPROFOR) to protect safe havens in an effort to stabilise the situation so that peace talks could ensue. UNPROFOR consisted of almost 40,000 personnel from thirty-nine different countries, including the United Kingdom, although the number of personnel involved would double as time went by. Theirs was no easy task as they regularly came under fire and NATO aircraft acting for UNPROFOR were employed to shoot down warplanes in the 'no-fly' zones or bombard aggressors elsewhere.

RIGHT: THERE WAS REALLY NO EXCUSE FOR GETTING LOST IN SARAJEVO.

The United Nations declared six safe havens in Bosnia to protect Muslim communities. By July 1995, Serbian forces had launched attacks against all of these, including Sarajevo. To the embarrassment of the UN forces, two of these areas fell under Serbian control, resulting in deplorable human rights atrocities by the Serbs. By December 1995, the warring factions had been brought back to the negotiating table and an uneasy peace was achieved.

Elements of the AAC were deployed to the Balkans as part of UNPROFOR, then IFOR, the NATO-led 'Implementation Force' in 1995 and SFOR, the 'Stabilisation Force' that took over from IFOR in 1996. The AAC operated variously from a base in the Croatian port of Split, from Ploce on the strip of Croatian coast that separates Bosnia and Herzegovina from the sea as well as flying from a forward base at Banja Luka, the second largest city in Bosnia and Herzegovina after Sarajevo. Captain Tom O'Malley was a Lynx pilot in the Balkans; 'We had two main roles there,' recalled Captain O'Malley. 'One was as the liaison with the higher echelons of the multi-national division, moving the generals and their entourages around from A to B. But we also had a war fighting role and we were equipped for anti-armour operations using the TOW system.

'The beauty of the Lynx is that you can take the missiles off and fly it as a utility helicopter. Obviously we used to change the equipment depending on what the task was. The routine tasking

ABOVE: WEATHER CONDITIONS IN THE BALKANS COULD BE TRULY TESTING.

LEFT: 3 REGIMENT PRIOR TO UN DEPLOYMENT TO PLOCE IN 1995.

RIGHT: STEPHANIE AND MATTHEW WELCOME HOME THEIR DAD,
SERGEANT RICHIE BUTLER, WHEN 3 REGIMENT RETURNED FROM PLOCE
TO WATTISHAM IN OCTOBER 1995.

was to move personnel around safely and quickly. We were not affected by the landmine threat they would face on the roads, and many of the roads were in a state of disrepair in any case. That was a good, exciting tour.'

The situation in the Balkans was, nonetheless, extremely complicated and extremely dangerous. There were many deaths among the personnel of the international force, including the British, and the AAC suffered its first four fatalities in August 1995 when Sergeant Martin Osborne, Corporal Ian Macdonald, Air Trooper Graham Witherstone and Air Trooper Roger Willingale died in a Lynx crash near Ploce. Sadly, they were not to be the last.

CHAPTER EIGHT

ECHOES FROM THE PAST
1997 – 2007

M ajor changes to the way that the AAC trains its pilots came about in 1997 with the founding of the Defence Helicopter Flying School. This was a joint venture between a private company, FBS Limited, and the Ministry of Defence. The new training facility was established at RAF Shawbury, where all helicopter pilots from the Army, RAF and Royal Navy were to receive their initial helicopter flying training. FBS Limited and its associate company, FB Heliservices, were engaged to supply and maintain the Squirrel helicopters that were to be used as the standard training aircraft as well as contributing more than a third of the flying instructors.

If such a large delegation of responsibility to a contractor outside of the armed forces seems a little unusual at first glance, it should be noted that the AAC, in common with the other armed services, has always maintained very close links with its helicopter suppliers. In 1956 Mr Coombs from Westland accompanied the JHU when they went in to Suez, and in 1982 Westland engineers worked with REME personnel to design and install mountings on the Gazelle for rocket pods prior to deployment in the Falklands. FB Heliservices can, in fact, claim a far longer association with the

Corps than their mere ten years' involvement with the DHFS. Bristow Helicopters is one of the partners in FB Heliservices and two of their employees recently celebrated forty years of continuous service working on the School of Army Aviation fleet at Middle Wallop.

INITIAL HELICOPTER FLYING TRAINING FOR AAC PILOTS IS ON THE WESTLAND SQUIRREL AT THE DEFENCE HELICOPTER TRAINING SCHOOL AT RAF SHAWBURY.

ABOVE: A BELL 212 OF 25 FLIGHT EMBARKS A PATROL ON A HILLTOP CLEARING IN THE JUNGLES OF BELIZE.

The ten Squirrels used for the Operational Training Phase of the Army Pilots Course at Middle Wallop are supplied and maintained by FB Heliservices as is a Bell 212 used for aircrew training prior to postings to Belize or Brunei where the company is also contracted to provide the Bell 212 for AAC use. The twin-engined Bell 212, developed from the single-engined Bell 205, more popularly known as the 'Huey', is a remarkably versatile aircraft ideally suited to the hot and humid jungles of both Belize and Brunei. In Belize, 25 Flight AAC flies three Bell 212s in support of BATSUB (British Army Training Support Unit Belize), providing troop transport, tactical supply and casualty evacuation, the side-mounted winch being of particular benefit in the recovery of casualties from difficult jungle or mountain terrain.

In Brunei three further Bell 212s are flown by 7 Flight, supporting jungle training exercises throughout the region. Although never intended to be a deployable unit, through sheer hard work and a little ingenuity, 7 Flight and their FB Heliservices engineers turned themselves into a rapid reaction force when the Boxing Day Tsunami devastated coastal communities around the Indian Ocean in 2004.

When news of the worst natural disaster for two hundred years first broke, many of 7 Flight's personnel were on holiday, scattered around the Far East. They immediately began phoning in to ask when the flight would be leaving to lend a hand. Wheels were already in motion. With the agreement of The Sultan of Brunei, the British Government offered the Indonesians the assistance of the Brunei Garrison in relief operations. Helicopter support was requested by the Indonesians and 7 Flight's OC, Major Peter Suddards, along with FB Heliservices Deputy Chief Engineer in Bruei, Mr Phil Brown set off for Banda Aceh at the northern tip of Sumatra as a reconnaissance/advance party.

Meanwhile, 7 Flight's base at Serai was a hive of activity. A massive effort from all involved had the flight ready to move within five days. An RAF C-17 was loaded with a fully laden 4 ton

ABOVE: ONE OF 25 FLIGHT'S BELL 212S PASSING THE ANCIENT MAYAN TEMPLE OF CARACOL IN BELIZE.

Bedford, a 1-ton water trailer, an FFR Land Rover, a 4x4 Toyota Prado, seventeen passengers and two Bell 212s.

On arrival at Banda Aceh, where their accommodation was sited in a swamp close to the airfield's main runway, they were ready to begin operations within twenty-four hours. Working and living conditions at Banda Aceh were far from perfect. The airfield had become one of the busiest aviation zones in the world with up to 500 helicopter moves each day and 100 fixed wing flights. The continual noise was horrendous as was the temperature at around 40°C with 85% humidity. Monsoon rains kept the swamp very

much a swamp, but 7 Flight's personnel and the FB Heliservices engineers kept both aircraft working up to ten hours a day.

Four flight crews alternated morning and afternoon sorties lifting between 12,000 and 15,000 lbs of aid each day. It was sorely needed in places like Lamno, a town in their west coast area of operations that had once been home to 24,000 people. It now had 6,000 dead, 12,000 displaced with around 3,000 orphaned children among them. Providing the aid that the tsunami survivors so desperately needed was often a perilous task. Captain John Bushell later wrote; 'On one particular occasion the aircraft

ABOVE: LEARNING HOW TO SPLINT A BADLY BROKEN LEG DURING GROUND TRAINING AT MIDDLE WALLOP.

RIGHT: SIGNALS TRAINING AT MIDDLE WALLOP, WHERE 2 REGIMENT TRAINS SOLDIERS WHO HAVE ALREADY GONE THROUGH THE ARMY'S BASIC TRAINING PROGRAMME.

BELOW: SOLDIERS WHO HAVE PASSED THE RAF'S AIRCREW SELECTION TESTS THEN FACE THE ARMY FLYING GRADING COURSE WHICH INCLUDES THIRTEEN HOURS IN THE SLINGSBY FIREFLY.

163

1997 – 2007

were fully laden, the weather started to turn and the lead crew decided that both aircraft should initially land and wait it out. The site chosen was completely clear but on landing the first aircraft was mobbed by hundreds of people within seconds.

'The people were so hungry for food they fought each other viciously to grab anything they could. They did anything to get at the aircraft, often not aware of the danger they were in. LCpl Davey Allardyce just managed to rugby tackle two children who were about to run into the tail rotor and kill themselves. The aircraft

troubles. Having seen this, the second crew into this site sensibly stayed in the air and threw everything out from about 15 feet, but the ensuing fight for food was not pleasant to watch.'

During the five-week deployment, 7 Flight's two Bell 212s flew 209 missions, including seven serious casualty evacuations, supplying 244,100 lbs of medical supplies, equipment and food . It was an effort of which the entire AAC can justifiably be immensely proud.

The involvement of FB Heliservices and the creation of DHFS

couldn't take off because people were swarming all over it. The pilot, Sgt Kief Khanlarian RE, had to get out of the aircraft to replace LCpl Allardyce (who had now stationed himself at the tail rotor) to drag people out of the aircraft who had clambered in to rip open the boxes.

'Mr Pete Bird (aircraft engineer) was being mobbed on the other side of the aircraft and was trying to maintain some control of the distribution of aid but getting a good beating for his

ABOVE: FEMALE SOLDIERS ARE NOW DOING EVERY JOB IMAGINABLE IN THE AAC FROM STANDING GUARD TO FLYING HELICOPTERS.

allowed the Corps to concentrate its own resources on training personnel for the ever more specialised roles required of them. Middle Wallop, Headquarters of the Director of Army Aviation since 1970, is also home to the School of Army Aviation where 2 Regiment conducts ground training, taking soldiers who have

'. . . WE'RE LIKE GREMLINS – POUR SOME WATER ON A COUPLE OF US AND WE'LL GET EVERYWHERE . . .'

completed basic training through Phase 2 'special to arms' training and later Phase 3 career progression courses. All AAC soldiers, whatever specialist skills they may hope to acquire in the Corps, must be trained as soldiers first and foremost. They receive basic training at the Army Training Regiment in Winchester, but must also be able to drive military vehicles, for which they train initially at the Defence School of Transport at Leconfield.

When they return to Middle Wallop, they are taught how to operate and maintain tactical radios; marshal, refuel and rearm

Flying training is conducted at Middle Wallop by the Flying Wing which takes would-be pilots who have passed the Aircrew Selection Tests at RAF College Cranwell, through a demanding Army Flying Grading course – three weeks and 13 hours in a bright yellow Slingsby Firefly 160 to identify whether candidates have the aptitude to become an Army pilot. Later, once they have learned the basics of helicopter flying, students spend eighteen weeks at Middle Wallop on Operational Training to learn how to fly as an Army pilot before Conversion to Type training – nine weeks

ABOVE: SETTING A GAZELLE UP ON ITS 'ROLLER SKATES' TO TOW IT TO THE HANGAR AREA AT RAF ALDERGROVE IN NORTHERN IRELAND.

aircraft; set up and defend helicopter landing sites and a host of other tasks. Yet, despite any acquired technical expertise, they remain soldiers. As Lieutenant-Colonel Paul Beaver noted, 'Last year [2006] several senior NCOs were posted to Afghanistan to train the Afghan National Army and found themselves leading them into combat . . . it is clear that they are soldiers first – and that's how it should be.'

learning to handle the aircraft they will be expected to fly when posted to their regiments. Once posted, they will undergo a Conversion to Role course with their regiment to bring them up to combat-ready status.

Over the past ten years, there has also been an upsurge in the numbers of women joining the AAC. Female personnel now take their place alongside their male colleagues at all levels within the AAC – on guard duty, in ground crews or as specialists in signals or logistics. Unique within the British Army, women in the AAC are also involved in a direct combat role. Female pilots fly exactly

SPECIFICATION

→ Engine	Caterpillar C-12 electronic control, 6-cylinder in-line, turbo charged and aftercooled
→ Engine capacity	11.9 litres
→ Maximum power output	445 HP at 1700 rpm
→ Peak torque	2,101 Nm (1,550 ft-lb) at 1200 rpm
→ Transmission	Full-time all-wheel drive
→ Armament	Cab can be fitted with 7.62 mm machine gun
→ Overall height	11 feet 6 inches (3.5 m)
→ Overall width	8 feet 3 inches (2.5 m)
→ Overall length (inc trailer)	49 feet 6 inches (15 m)
→ Tanker payload	20,000 litres fuel or 18,000 litres water
→ Crew	2

OSHKOSH WHEELED TANKER

'THIS WILL GIVE OUR FORCES ONE OF THE MOST ADVANCED
WHEELED TANKER FLEETS IN THE WORLD . . .'

LORD BACH, DEFENSE PRECUREMENT MINISTER

The Oshkosh Truck Corporation, which takes its name from the town of Oshkosh in Wisconsin that has been home to the company for over a century, was commissioned by the MOD in 2003 to supply 357 wheeled tankers, the last unit being delivered towards the end of 2006. The tanker order consisted of 218 Close Support Tankers (Fuel), 57 Close Support Tankers (Water) and 82 Tactical Aircraft Refuellers. The Oshkosh plant at Llantrisant near Cardiff was involved in the assembly of the vehicles, with the pumping modules supplied by Alfons Haar of Germany and the tanker trailers coming from Magyar of France. The tractor unit, built by Oshkosh in America, is common to all three versions of the tanker.

Powered by an 11.9 litre Caterpillar engine, the tractor unit has permanent six-wheel drive, a central tyre inflation system and a run-flat function that provides continuous air to a puncture. The cab accommodates a driver and passenger with room for an occasional third occupant and sleeping bunks for a crew of two. The windscreen, roof, side walls and door frames can all be folded down to reduce the cab height for loading onto aircraft. Having first entered service with the Royal Logistics Corps in 2005, the Oshkosh has been deployed on operations in both Iraq and Afghanistan.

ABOVE: A LYNX FROM 4 REGIMENT IS LOADED ONTO AN ANTONOV AN-124 AT BRIZE NORTON IN 1999 TO FLY OUT TO THE FORMER YUGOSLAVIA.

RIGHT: A LYNX USING THE 'CHEDDAR GORGE' BAD WEATHER ROUTE THROUGH THE MOUNTAINS SOUTH OF BANJA LUKA.

the same sort of missions as their male counterparts. This is a far cry from the days when, almost a century ago, WAACs with the RFC held no official service rank, but the big changes have really only come within the last few years.

Staff Sergeant Lambert is an AH Crypto Custodian, handling secret codes for the Apache and is also a communications instructor. She has been in the AAC for sixteen years. 'When I initially joined,' she recalled, 'there were only about seven or eight females in my intake. We never had any real problems with that, although it could be difficult being the only female around. When we were sent out to our regiments, we shared accommodation with the guys, even bathroom facilities, but we couldn't afford to be precious about that and we never asked for special treatment. We were soldiers and we knew we just had to get on with it.'

After sixteen years, Lambert is the only one of her contemporaries still in the Army.

'Things changed for a lot of the girls. They got married, they had kids and the Army was no longer the lifestyle for them. But there are more women in the AAC now than ever before. There are

another echo from the past, from the time when the Army, Navy and RAF worked together under the auspices of the JEHU, the JHC was created to bring together the different expertise and skills of the three services' air and ground crews, uniting their battlefield helicopters for operations under one command. The services, naturally, had always worked in close cooperation on exercise and on operations. The AAC flew out of Aldergrove in Northern Ireland alongside RAF and Naval helicopters and never was that cooperation more apparent than during the Falklands campaign.

females doing every job you can imagine. We're like Gremlins – pour some water on a couple of us and we'll get everywhere. Just don't feed us after midnight!'

At the time of writing, Staff Sergeant Lambert was delighted to be expecting her first child, but fully intended to return to duty after the birth. Never have experience and expertise such as hers, the skills and training of all of the AAC's personnel, been in greater demand than they have in the past ten years, especially since the formation of the Joint Helicopter Command in 1999. Like

LYNX GUNSHIPS, NOT UNLIKE THESE WERE USED TO GREAT EFFECT ON OPERATION BARRAS IN 2000.

The JHC was not, however, looking back towards the JEHU, but laying the foundations for future tri-service operations. Many such operations lay ahead.

AAC deployment in the Balkans and the former states of Yugoslavia, which began in 1994, was extended to Macedonia and Kosovo in the late 1990s and was to continue up to 2006. Flying

ABOVE: THE AAC'S NEWEST HELICOPTER, THE APACHE AH1 'LONGBOW' DWARFTS THE AAC'S FIRST HELICOPTER, THE SKEETER.

conditions in the Balkans were often far from perfect, with swiftly changing weather in the mountains adding to the constant threat of attack from the ground, many of the different factions involved in the conflict more than ready to take a pot shot at a passing helicopter. Sadly, flying accidents claimed a number of lives. Captain Philip Jarvis and Lance Corporal Christopher Addis, along with REME Sergeant David Kinsley, died as a result of a Lynx crash outside the Gorni Vakuf base west of Sarajevo just before Christmas 1998, while Captain Andrew Crous, flying an RAF Puma, and Flight Lieutenant Mark Maguire both died when their Puma crashed in appalling weather in the mountains near the Macedonian border in April 2001.

The risks involved in certain aspects of Army flying can be substantial, not least when the services of AAC personnel are required in far from ordinary situations. In August 2000, two Lynx from 657 Squadron were involved in a daring rescue mission

in Sierra Leone when eleven soldiers from the Royal Irish Regiment were taken prisoner by a renegade militia unit known as the 'West Side Boys'. The British soldiers were taken hostage along with their military liaison from Sierra Leone, while working as part of a team training the government army in the country. In return for the release of the hostages, the West Side Boys demanded the release from custody of their leader, General Papa, as well as medical and food supplies.

Six days after their initial capture, five of the hostages were released in return for medical supplies and a satellite telephone. The remaining seven continued to be held at the West Side Boys' camp at Geri Bana on the banks of the Rokel Creek, an area of dense jungle vegetation. The Royal Irish group's three Land-

ABOVE: TECHNOLOGICAL ADVANCES IN THE AIR HAVE NEVER HAD ANY EFFECT ON CERTAIN ASPECTS OF TRAINING ON THE GROUND . . .

ABOVE, RIGHT: AAC PERSONNEL ON THE GROUND AND IN THE AIR DEVELOPED A HUGE SENSE OF PRIDE IN THE APACHE WHILE TRAINING TO GO OPERATIONAL.

RIGHT: THE SAME SENSE OF PRIDE IN ACHIEVEMENT HAS TO APPLY TO MORE THE MORE TRADITIONAL TASKS OF A SOLDIER.

Rovers, equipped with heavy machine guns, were located at another West Side Boys' base on the river a few hundred metres away. All of this was reported back by covert SAS observation teams as negotiations with the kidnappers continued. On 5 September, eleven days after the British soldiers were taken, a contingent from 1 Para arrived in Senegal to prepare for armed intervention in the hostage crisis. When the SAS covert teams reported that the West Side Boys were staging mock executions and appeared to be considering a move to even more remote hill country, the decision was taken to implement the rescue plan.

Just after 6 am on 10 September, three Chinooks and the two AAC Lynx took off from Freetown airport, accompanied by a locally-operated Hind. They headed inland towards Rokel Creek. After fifteen minutes flying at treetop height with the Lynx leading the way, they reached their target area. The two Lynx peeled off, approaching the camps from different directions before strafing the river banks with their machine guns while the Chinooks set down the assault force. The SAS concentrated on securing the hostages while the Paras took on the West Side Boys. The six British soldiers and the Sierra Leonean lieutenant were quickly whisked to safety as a vicious firefight erupted. Twelve of the rescuers were wounded, one seriously, and one SAS man was killed. At least twenty-five West Siders were killed and eighteen were captured, including their leader, Foday Kallay. The three Land-Rovers were also recovered. For his part in the action, AAC Captain Allan Moyes was awarded the Distinguished Flying Cross.

The AAC went into the new millennium with the prospect of an awesome new weapon to add to their arsenal. The Apache AH1 'Longbow' had been

ordered in 1995 and the first aircraft had arrived from Boeing in America in 1999. The first Apache built by Westland at their Yeovil plant was delivered in July 2000. Deliveries were to roll on from there, a total of eight Apaches being built for the AAC in America and a further fifty-nine coming from Westland, the final aircraft being delivered in 2004.

Developed from the Apache AH-64 that has been in service with the US Army since 1984, the Longbow Apache, so-called because of the cheese-shaped dome carrying the Northrop Grumman Longbow radar on the main rotor mast, uses Rolls-Royce engines that generate up to 25 per cent more power than the standard General Electric units. It is the first pure attack helicopter ever utilised by the AAC. Its Hellfire guided missiles, CRV7 rocket pods and 30 mm chain gun provide it with the most formidable firepower of any aircraft the Corps has ever sent aloft but it is the sophistication of the Apache's electronic systems that make it such a remarkable machine. The Longbow radar can simultaneously detect up to 256 different targets and prioritise them according to their speed and direction. It can do this day or night, in all types of weather, its systems allowing a pair of Apaches working together to dominate an area the size of Salisbury Plain.

The imminent arrival of the Apache meant that a great deal of retraining had to be undertaken both in the UK and, as it transpired, in the US. Captain Tom O'Malley had been a Lynx instructor for two years when he was sent across the Atlantic to retrain on Apaches in January 2002. 'A group of us were sent to Fort Rucker in Alabama through until mid May,' he recalled. 'It's no secret that our simulator at Middle Wallop wasn't working as it

LEFT: CARTOONS LIKE THESE APPEARED ON NOTICE BOARDS IN HANGARS TO REMIND EVERYONE THAT WORKING ON THE GROUND WAS EVERY BIT AS DANGEROUS AS TAKING TO THE AIR.

should. It just wasn't ready in time. We had to have Apache in service by 2005. A lot of defence assumptions were made based on the fact that Apache would be ready by then. So, to make up lost time, sixteen pilots, mostly instructors, were selected to go to Fort Rucker.

'When we got back from America, we set up the school at Middle Wallop, received the first aircraft, and set up what is now 673 Squadron. I taught up until February 2004 before moving to Dishforth AMTAT, Air Manouevre Training and Advisory Team, where pilots and ground crews were taught to integrate the Apache into the all-arms battle, along with people like Forward Observation Officers, so that they knew, and could then teach, how best to call for fire from an Apache.

'There's an immense amount of pride in being associated with the aircraft. Everybody in the Army is convinced that it will do what it is expected do. It is crash survivable. It has armour plating all round the cockpit to protect the aircrew. It's got a defensive aids suite which will defeat any of the known threats on the market

today. It will take a hit and continue to fly – and that's been proven in combat not only by us but by the Americans before us. Everybody has a great deal of confidence in the aircraft.'

While preparations continued to bring the Apache up to operational status, the AAC continued to fulfil its other commitments all over the world, including Operation Herrick. In 2001, following the 9/11 attacks in the United States, the Americans demanded that the Taliban government in Afghanistan hand over al-Qaeda leader Osama bin Laden, known to have been hiding in the country since 1996 under the protection of the Taliban. Al-Qaeda had been behind a number of attacks on US personnel over the preceding years and had acknowledged their own involvement in the 9/11 attacks. Their bases in Afghanistan had previously been hit by the US in retaliatory missile strikes, but the 9/11 atrocities gave added impetus to the international 'war

'. . . WE CAME TO THE CONCLUSION THAT IF WE HAD TO DITCH IN THE SEA WE WOULD BE MEETING OUR MAKER!'

ABOVE: ALTHOUGH NEVER DESIGNED TO GO TO SEA, THE AAC APACHE CONDUCTED SUCCESSFUL DECK LANDING TRIALS ABOARD HMS *OCEAN* IN 2005.

on terror'. America called for the release of foreign nationals held by the Taliban, the arrest of terrorists known to be based there and the closure of their camps. When negotiations failed to bear fruit, the Americans, with support from Britain, the Afghan Northern Alliance and, later, UN forces, took direct military action against the Taliban. Air attacks commenced on 7 October 2001 and coalition forces were soon operating on the ground along with troops of the ANA. Operation Herrick is the codename under which the continuing British involvement in Aghanistan has been conducted since 2002.

As the situation in Afghanistan developed, Lance Corporal Ben Jones found himself on exercise in Kenya, working with Gazelle ground crew. 'We went to Kenya for six weeks on exercise before converting to type on Apache,' he explained. 'It really is beautiful out there. We were supporting the infantry, standing by for casualty evacuation, doing range clearances in the morning, making sure there was no wildlife around before the artillery started firing on the ranges. We were in tents and there were plenty of bugs around – hornets and things they called camel spiders. Anything like that seemed to be about ten times bigger over there!'

Often described as having an insect-like appearance, the Apache was the 'Ugly Bug' with which Ben Jones began training on his return to Dishforth. As a Landing Point Commander he was in charge of the Apache's seven-man ground crew. 'It's not the prettiest helicopter in the world,' he admitted, 'but it's probably the most advanced. There's a lot more work for us on the Apache than on the Lynx. We need a lot more manpower and equipment, more vehicles and extra stores. On Lynx all we were really working with were the TOW missiles, but on Apache we've got Hellfire, CRV 7 rockets, 30 mm cannon rounds, chaff, flares – it's a much bigger job altogether.'

Training exercises with the new aircraft were ultimately to include a series of trials aboard HMS *Ocean* in 2005. In yet another echo from the past, it was a previous HMS *Ocean* which first carried AAC helicopters to war in Suez in 1956. The new Clyde-built vessel was commissioned in 1998 as a helicopter assault ship, regularly carrying Sea King and Lynx helicopters. The Apache air and ground crews took some time to get used to the idea of operating on board ship.

'HMS *Ocean* was a bit different,' admitted Ben Jones. 'We had to figure out how we would work with our ammunition on deck. Everything has to be strapped down. Accommodation was quite weird. We had three bunk beds, one on top of the other, and you've not got much space. We were on for two weeks at first but when we went back on board we took far less kit with us.'

A lack of space aboard ship was the least of the worries faced by the air crews.

'The navy pilots were all quite receptive to the Apache,' said Tom O'Malley, 'and they admired our courage in flying an aircraft that was never designed to go to sea. Unlike the Sea King or Lynx which have flotation bags to keep the aircraft afloat in the sea to allow the aircrew to escape, we have armour plate. The Apache would be like a brick in the sea. Also, each cockpit has only one door. It has an explosive charge around the Perspex, but if that fails to detonate then you are pretty much trapped. We did underwater escape training, watched a very scary video and we came to the conclusion that if we had to ditch in the sea we would be meeting our maker!'

It was while aboard HMS *Ocean* that the Apache teams learned that they would be going to Afghanistan. 'We left HMS *Ocean* earlier than planned to go to Oman for pre-deployment training and live firing exercises,' recalled Tom O'Malley. 'We thought that we would go straight from Oman out to Afghanistan but the

ABOVE: APACHE LIVE FIRE EXERCISES WERE CONDUCTED IN OMAN PRIOR TO DEPLOYMENT TO AFGHANISTAN.

political situation delayed our deployment so we came home for a month or so first.'

Ben Jones recalls arriving in Afghanistan in April 2006. 'We were the first [British] Apache squadron to go out there so we had to set everything up and figure out how everything was going to work. It took about a month to get into the swing of things. We saw the thermometer hit fifty-nine degrees. At that point, you move a finger and the sweat is just pouring off you.'

The Royal Engineers who had built the Joint Helicopter Command's forward operating base, Camp Bastion, had laboured hard in the heat and dust of the mountains at an altitude of 3,000 feet. Everything had to be done in daylight hours rather than in the cool of the evening because work lamps at night would have made them such tempting targets for anyone lurking on a hillside in the darkness. Not only had they to avoid sunburn but also burns from any metal with which they were working as the direct sunshine left it too hot to handle.

Despite the heat, and the fine, powder-like dust that permeated clothes and equipment, the ground crews, engineers and technicians had the first Apaches ready for their inaugural combat operations in good time. 'We went operational three days before we were expected to,' Tom O'Malley remembered, 'which is testament to the men who had to make all of the preparations on the ground.

look like a walk in the park. Afghanistan was true war fighting in its rawest sense. Operation Herrick is a peace support operation but actually, for the guys on the ground faced with a hardened enemy who will fight to the death, it is fixed bayonets and hand-to-hand fighting on occasion.

'Providing close-in fire support for those troops was a real eye

DURING THE WINTER OF 2006, 4 REGIMENT TOOK PART IN EXERCISE CLOCKWORK TIN NORWAY TO PREPARE FOR THE EXTREME COLD THEY COULD FACE WHEN DEPLOYED EITHER TO THE BALKANS OR AFGHANISTAN.

opener because up until that point we would go to a gunnery range with the nearest ground troops around five hundred metres away for safety reasons. Very quickly we were engaging enemy positions with the cannon less than fifty metres from our troops. We had never done anything as close as that but the alternative was to say, "You are too close to the enemy. I can't fire." They could then be overwhelmed and that's just not going to happen.

'What did have to happen was that the stand-off distance – my distance from the target in order to maintain a degree of safety for the aircraft – had to be reduced. We can employ our cannon up a

It wasn't long before we were engaged in combat, supporting ground troops, initially working very closely with the Canadians who don't have their own attack helicopters.

'Afghanistan made my other operational deployments – a couple of tours in Northern Ireland, a couple of tours in Bosnia –

ABOVE: AN APACHE OF 9 REGIMENT ON A DESERT TRAINING FLIGHT PRIOR TO DEPLOYMENT IN AFGHANISTAN.

BELOW: AN APACHE OF 656 SQUADRON ON THE DISPERSAL AREA AT CAMP BASTION IN AFGHANISTAN.

ABOVE: THERE WAS NO SHORTAGE OF VOLUNTEERS FROM AMONG THE MARINES OF ZULU COMPANY TO RIDE ON THE OUTSIDE OF THE APACHES.

range of four kilometres, although they are far more accurate at two kilometres. In practice, in order to give the ground troops the cover they needed, we had to get much closer. For a rifleman, a thousand metres might seem like a long way off, but for us it's almost point blank.'

As well as operating with the Canadians, the AAC Apaches supported 3 Para. 'When we were speaking to the paras in the cookhouse,' recalled Ben Jones, 'they all told us how grateful they were to have an Apache on their shoulder when they were out on patrols and they came into contact with the enemy. They said it had saved their lives on numerous occasions. That makes you feel good. You know that the job you are doing is making a difference.

'When they were out on a mission we would have two Apaches out and two on the deck, turning and burning. We'd be uploading them ready for when the other two came back. The Taliban know when the Apaches are up there. When they're not there they come out and start shooting. We knew we had to keep the Apaches there as long as we could.'

'The Taliban resisted at every twist and turn of the road,' Tom O'Malley recalled. 'They were tenacious. They never turned and fled. They would almost always stand and fight. We always worked in pairs to provide mutual support but we would split so as to provide fire support to two different formations, whether it be a company or platoon size, but still be within sight of each other at different sides of the battle area.

'The cannon was the weapon of choice because of its weight of fire and its accuracy. The rockets, while they packed a bigger punch, were less accurate and within the context of the fighting you would rarely have enough separation between friendly troops and the enemy to comfortably engage the enemy with the rockets safely. When push came to shove it was done, but that wasn't an easy decision to take. The other weapon, the Hellfire is pure precision. You put a crosshair on a target and the missile goes exactly where you point.

'We served with 3 Para on the first tour, came home in August, then went back to Afghanistan to work with 3 Commando in November for a Christmas tour, which didn't please many people, not least my wife and three children . . .'

Although the Apache crews found that the Marines operated

1997 – 2007

Intelligence indicated that this was an important headquarters and communications node for the Taliban and an attack was mounted in force with support from US B1 bombers and A10 ground attack aircraft, artillery, Scimitar light tanks, the Marines' own Viking vehicles and, of course, aviation support from the Apaches.

The Marines had to cross two water courses, one of them the Helmund River, in the pre-dawn darkness to reach the outer walls of the fort and, having done so, engage the enemy in an intense firefight. Eventually, having taken several casualties, they withdrew to regroup and it quickly became apparent that one of their number was missing. It transpired that Lance Corporal Matthew Ford had been shot leading his section forward and, in the smoke and darkness, had been left behind when the Marines withdrew.

'I was the patrol leader of the high readiness flight,' said Tom O'Malley, 'my aircraft callsign was Ugly Five-Zero.' As an Apache pair, we were asked to stay on target and use our sensors to locate the missing Marine. We found very quickly a British soldier, who appeared to be injured lying right next to the Jugroom Fort wall. Due to the heat signature, we had to assume that he was still alive and that he was a casualty in need of medical treatment. I was flying with a pilot called Geordie Armatage with a second Apache, callsign Ugly Five-One, in support. We did a very low pass at about 25 feet to try to get "eyes on" for two reasons: first so that we could see if he was mobile at all and second so that he would know in no uncertain terms that we knew where he was. It was important that he should know that somebody would be coming to get him soon.

'We were then told that we were to prevent the casualty, whom we then found out was Matthew Ford, from falling into enemy hands. The fight was still going on between the Taliban in the fort and the ground troops across the river. The enemy may not have known that Matthew Ford was lying there but they would soon have spotted him. There was a lot of movement inside the fort and

differently from the Paras, being a more mobile force, their job remained the same – to support the troops on the ground as they took the fight to the enemy. During one operation in January 2007, codenamed Glacier, the Marines mounted a major attack against a large, heavily defended walled village known as Jugroom Fort.

right next to where Matthew lay was a big hole in the wall that had been generated by a B1 bomber. Had any one of those Taliban fighters caught a glimpse of the human form there they would have gone and got him. I have no doubt about that. We engaged targets with eight Hellfire missiles, five hundred rounds of thirty-mil and a shedload of rockets.

'Geordie and I discussed the idea with the crew of Ugly Five-One that we could do a cheeky dash, land, pick up the casualty and take him home. We suggested it to the ground troops but it was cast aside as a cowboy idea that would never work.'

As the minutes ticked by, however, and the prospect of crossing and re-crossing the rivers in daylight under fire made a ground force rescue untenable, rescue by Apache began to look as if it might be the only viable option. Uglies Five-Zero and Five-One were running low on fuel and had very little time left on station. Tom O'Malley again pressed for permission to use his Apaches to pick up Matthew Ford. 'We then suggested that we could stage a rescue if we took four Marines. We asked for four volunteers who would ride in on the sides of our aircraft – obviously there are no spare seats – and we could drop them right beside the casualty they could pick him up and bring him back to one of the aircraft. Out of all of the options available to the commanders on the ground, this was their best chance. It was risky, but we went.

'We flew in under the support of a B1 bomber. The B1 dropped

'. . . IT WAS CAST ASIDE AS A COWBOY IDEA
THAT WOULD NEVER WORK'

APACHE AH MK 1

APACHE INSTRUCTOR WO2 CRAIG REDMAN HAS A 'WALK ROUND'
AS PART OF HIS PRE-FLIGHT CHECKS.

SPECIFICATION

→ Engines	2 x Rolls-Royce Turbomeca RTM 322 gas turbines		→ Total length	58 feet 3 inches (17.76 m)
→ Maximum Level Flight Speed	163 mph		→ Fuselage length	51 feet (15.54 m)
→ Never Exceed Speed	230 mph		→ Height	16 feet 3 inches (4.95 m)
→ Hover in-Ground Effect	4172 m		→ Wing Span	19 feet (5.79 m)
→ Hover out-Ground Effect	2889 m		→ Main Rotor Span	48 feet (14.63 m)
→ Armament	30mm M230 Automatic Chain Gun		→ Maximum weight	22,282 lb (10107 kg)
	Up to 16 Hellfire guided missiles		→ Typical Mission weight	17,637 lb (8000 kg)
	Up to 76 CRV 7 2.75-inch rockets			

'IT'S NOT THE PRETTIEST HELICOPTER IN THE WORLD BUT IT'S PROBABLY THE MOST ADVANCED.'

LANDING POINT COMMANDER, LANCE CORPORAL BEN JONES

In 2000, the first of 67 Apache AH Mk 1 attack helicopters entered service with the Corps. Based on the Boeing (formerly McDonnell Douglas) AH-64D Apache Longbow which was introduced to the US Army in 1998, the UK variant was built by AgustaWestland at their Yeovil plant using component parts supplied by Boeing and incorporates specific, state-of-the-art systems that make it a truly formidable fighting machine.

The Helicopter Integrated Defensive Aids System (HIDAS) identifies potential threats to the aircraft, combining threat data with threat location to classify those of highest priority and determine appropriate countermeasures based upon the aircraft's movements and the level of countermeasure resources. Another highly sophisticated system, TADS (Target Acquisition Designation Sight) allows the crew to view targets in both visual and thermal imaging modes. The system can store over 1000 targets in its memory, identify up to 256 separate targets and prioritise the 16 targets that pose the greatest threat to the aircraft.

ABOVE: A LYNX OF 3 REGIMENT TRAINING WITH 3 PARA PRIOR TO DEPLOYMENT ON OPERATION TELIC.

ABOVE: AN AAC LYNX WORKING IN COOPERATION WITH AN RAF REGIMENT VEHICLE PATROL SOUTH OF BASRA AIRPORT IN NOVEMBER 2003.

184

1997 – 2007

a two thousand pound bomb on a target about three hundred metres away to create a bit of a diversion. Under the smoke and the fallout from that bomb, we nipped in. The dust and everything else drifted across my landing site and I made the decision then that I would go inside the fort to give the other aircraft enough space outside.

'I knew we needed all four pairs of boots on the ground to give us the best chance of success. Unfortunately, my action disorientated the Marines on the outside of my aircraft. In the smoke and dust, they got off the aircraft but couldn't see the casualty because he was outside the wall. My pilot, Geordie, then said, "I'll take them. I'll show them where he is." He got out and left me inside the fort on my own.

'A second Apache flight had now arrived and they were providing fire support for me. I was directing them, but they were also detecting movements and engaging targets independently. Jugroom was a large complex – the area where I landed between inner and outer walls was more than half the size of a football pitch. Landing inside the fort actually helped keep the Taliban at their inner wall defences and away from the breach.

'Outside they were being engaged by the Taliban using small arms. The front seat pilot saw that his two Marines were struggling with the casualty and, just before my rescue party appeared from inside the fort, he got out to help. When the other three arrived, the

six of them were easily able to handle the casualty but they were now coming under heavy fire.

'The whole thing took about five minutes. We had a couple of minutes where we had the element of surprise and it was relatively quiet. After that, it was non-stop. The two cover aircraft, Uglies Five-Two and Five-Three, were constantly engaging targets because, while the Apache is quick, it is also noisy and we obviously attracted attention while we were on the ground.

'The pilot of Ugly Five-One, inside the cockpit of the Apache outside the fort, then raised his collective lever so as to generate a dust screen to help conceal the rescue party.

Once they had secured the casualty to the other aircraft the three "ground party" from my aircraft made their way back and we made a dash back across the river.

'When we flew back to Camp Bastion, the ground crews were there to greet us and I said, "I don't think we'll be going anywhere for a while. I'm sure we've been hit." But they checked over the aircraft and there was not a single hole – not one. It was quite a morning, but we were all very upset when we discovered that Matthew had died from his injuries.'

For their actions at Jugroom, Tom O'Malley was awarded the DFC and Geordie Armatage the MC. The crew of Apache Ugly Five-One were also rewarded for their actions with an MC and a Joint

Commander's Commendation for bravery.

Even though they are responsible for fielding some of the most technologically advanced equipment in the world, sometimes the soldiers of the ultra-modern AAC must still rough it with low-tech facilities and living conditions. While the Apache would be something of a miracle machine to their forebears, the field conditions under which today's AAC personnel must occasionally operate would be entirely familiar to all of those who have served in the Corps over the past fifty years and beyond. This was never more apparent than during Operation Telic, the British codename for the invasion of Iraq, was launched to eliminate the perceived threat to world peace posed by Saddam Hussein's regime. Telic is a word which describes an act with meaning or purpose, although to most of the British Army it came to be yet another acronym, this time standing for Tell Everyone Leave Is Cancelled. Even operational codenames like Telic are concocted by high-tech computers nowadays, but when the AAC went back to Iraq in the form of 3 Regiment, sophisticated equipment did not, at first, extend as far as the soldiers' primitive living conditions. At times these would have been like a home-from-home for the soldiers of the AOP and Glider Pilot Regiment who served in the deserts of North Africa sixty years before.

Sergeants Lord and 'Turkish' Wilkins remembered enduring the heat and the dust of the twenty-first century desert war in Iraq. 'Most people at home don't really realise,' said Lord, 'that in those circumstances we had thousands of people living not only with no newspapers or showers but with no hot water at all and no cold water either – no cold drinking water.'

Wilkins found that our American brothers-in-arms were more than sympathetic. 'We came across an American refrigerated container,' he recalled. 'It was filled with bottles of cold water – so cold they had ice floating in them. We spent nearly half a day there just drinking lovely cold water.'

'A lot of us were in seventy-two-man tents with ninety-six sleeping in them. Going for a pee, you had to be careful finding your way out in the dark. Then you had the added problem of finding the latrine trench without walking straight up to it and falling in.' Sergeant Andrews of the GPR, sheltering under his olive tree in North Africa in 1943 prior to the invasion of Sicily, would have understood exactly how they felt.

The Apache was not yet ready to go to war but 3 Regiment

RIGHT: AAC SOLDIERS ON GUARD DUTY AS THE IRAQI DESERT BLOWS UP ONE OF ITS MANY DUST STORMS.

most certainly was. Following four weeks intensive desert training they were ready to deploy in March as part of the 46,000-strong British contingent of the international invasion force. The regiment was to operate their tried-and-tested, battle-proven combination of Lynx and Gazelle and was to take control of a vast expanse of desert around the Rumalyah oil field. During one phase of Operation Telic– with 3 Regiment at the heart of the tactical 'Air Manoeuvre' deployment concept which involves an all-arm aviation battlegroup including army aviation, infantry, artillery, engineers and support helicopters - CO Lieutenant Colonel George Butler had responsibility for an Area of Operations (AO) of about 6,000km2. It was probably the largest battlegroup AO in history.

Initially, 3 Regiment's job was to guard against a breakout of the Irqi 51st Mechanised Division, although this never actually happened. Later, their routine tasks included supplying security for US Forces within the AO and on the main supply route, although their main job was, as always, to support 16 Air Assault Brigade. AAC aircraft came under fire on many occasions before the regiment was finally given the opportunity to strike back.

Shortly after midnight on the morning of 26 March two Lynx of 662 Squadron took off to attack a target in Basra. Bombing and artillery fire had failed to eliminate determined opposition in a factory complex which lay two kilometres forward of Bridge 4

ABOVE: TWO OF 659 SQUADRON'S LYNX ARRIVING BACK AT BASRA AIRPORT FOLLOWING A SORTIE OVER SOUTHERN IRAQ.

RIGHT: EYES, FACE AND, MOST IMPORTANTLY, WEAPON NEEDED TO BE SHIELDED AGAINST THE DESERT DUST.

over the Shatt al Basra. The bridge was held by the Black Watch and friendly Challenger tanks were identified close by on the right bank as the aircraft approached with the fires of battle blazing on the Basra skyline. The Lynx crewed by WO1 John Tymon and the Squadron OC Major Crispin Orr had the honour of firing the first Lynx TOW of the conflict. Captain Neil Passmore and WO2 Del Clements in the second Lynx fired seconds later and between them the two aircraft released seven missiles, guiding the missiles under a set of high voltage electricity lines on to their targets. Captain Passmore later reported that 'TOW can be fired from the ten foot hover, beneath a 150ft set of wires onto a target two kilometres away, with no problems at all . . . if the missiles hit a mortar ammunition dump, the secondary explosions are most impressive . . .'

Two days later the Lynx crews of 662 Squadron were involved in a different kind of action in Basra. Enemy 'technicals' - pick-up trucks with heavy machine guns or mortars mounted on the flatbed - were driving through crowds of civilians who were attempting to flee Basra. They were firing on soldiers and vehicles at vehicle checkpoints as well as mowing down the civilians. When a pair of Lynx were despatched to deal with the problem, the technicals scattered, attempting to conceal themselves up sidestreets and behind buildings. Two of the vehicles, however,

were skilfully tracked by the Lynx crews and blown to pieces with TOW missiles.

On the same day, Lynx and Gazelle teams operating in support of an advance by 16 Air Assault Brigade near the North Rumaylah bridge responded to reports from Household Cavalry Scimitar reconnaissance crews who had sighted Iraqi armour. When they arrived on station, the Gazelles and Lynx were subject to artillery and mortar fire but engaged a variety of targets throughout the action. At one point one of the Gazelle pilots noted that tracer rounds were passing less than five metres over the top of an adjacent Gazelle's rotor disc. Despite poor visibility, eight missiles were fired, three fire missions were conducted from the Gazelles and at least two T-55 tanks, two 122mm self-propelled guns and a 120mm towed howitzer were destroyed.

Although the fighting in the south was over within a few days, there was still plenty of work for 3 Regiment's helicopter teams, helping in aid efforts for the civilian population and with the joint civil and military projects aimed at rebuilding Iraq's infrastructure. When the bulk of the battlegroup returned to the UK in June 2003, 662 Squadron remained behind to perform security and liaison duties in a country that continued to be rocked by violent unrest.

The AAC's involvement with the Joint Helicopter Force (Iraq)

ABOVE: 3 REGT AAC, MK 7 LYNX/TOW, OVER BASRA PALACE, SPRING 2003.

continues to this day, its personnel on the ground and in the air proving their professionalism and dedication under the most arduous of circumstances. There is no such thing as a 'routine' flight in Iraq. In November 2004 an AAC Lynx commanded by Captain Scottie Watkins was flying stores and personnel from Baghdad to the 1st Black Watch Battalion battlegroup at Camp Dogwood from where security operations were being mounted around Fallujah. The Lynx, piloted by Captain Keith Reesby, was flying in tandem with an RAF Puma. On their second stores run of the day, they had just crossed the Euphrates River when the Lynx was studded by small-arms fire. 'We heard a large explosion,' recalled Captain Watkins, 'as a 7.62mm round smashed its way through the pilot's door Perspex window. Debris, in the form of what I can only be described as a fine mist, appeared instantly in front of my pilot, Keith Reesby . . . The smell of cordite pervaded

and then there was a yell of pain and the realisation that one of the crew had been hit. It is a sound I will not soon forget.'

In fact, it was Keith Reesby who had been hit. Captain Watkins decided to return to Camp Dogwood and within minutes Keith Reesby was aboard an American Army Blackhawk on the way to hospital. Within an hour of being wounded, he was in surgery. Three months later, he was back flying again. There have been many such stories in Iraq, not all of which have had such happy endings. Sadly, Captain David Dobson and four others lost their lives when the Royal Navy Lynx he was flying was shot down over Basra in May 2006.

With eyes on the future, the Corps was heavily involved when the Ministry of Defence signed a £1 billion deal with AgustaWestland in June 2006, a Strategic Partnering Arrangement which secured future support for Britain's military

ABOVE: THE FUTURE LYNX WILL PROVIDE THE AAC WITH FORTY
BATTLEFIELD RECONNAISSANCE HELICOPTERS.

helicopter fleets, with a contract for the development of the Future Lynx as a mainstay of the Arrangement. Future Lynx will provide the AAC with forty Battlefield Reconnaissance Helicopters. Although it was originally intended that Future Lynx would replace the Lynx AH7 and AH9 utility aircraft still in service, it is now planned that it will be equipped to work alongside Apache and other battlefield weapons systems, relaying tactical and targeting information. A laser target designator and range finder mounted in a turret in the aircraft's nose, for example, will 'light up' targets for the Apache. Future Lynx will, however, have built-in provisions to allow for the capability of carrying a variety of weapons.

Future Lynx is scheduled to enter service with the AAC in 2014 and, although its capabilities will supplant some of the workload currently undertaken by the Lynx and Gazelle, by that time both of those aircraft will be of pensionable age, the Gazelle having entered service with the AAC in 1973 and the Lynx following four years later. A range of options is now being considered to cover the utility roles fulfilled by the Gazelle and Lynx in 2007.

In 2007, of course, the Army Air Corps celebrated its Golden Jubilee. The celebrations actually began somewhat prematurely with the first of a number of different events to mark the Jubilee starting in Portsmouth on 2 October 2006. Exercise Golden Eagle began when the sixty-seven-foot ocean going yacht *Challenger* set sail for an epic journey around the world. The 33,000 nautical miles were to be covered in ten stages, with a different crew of AAC personnel manning the yacht on each stage. Naturally, the reason *Challenger* began its voyage so early was because of the time it would take to journey around the world using only sail power. The yacht completed its voyage eleven months later in Gosport on 31 August 2007 – arriving home precisely on time for the AAC's Fiftieth Anniversary the next day.

Other celebratory events included Alps 4000 which involved four teams of climbers who came from all of the AAC regiments whose challenge was to climb fifty 4000 m peaks in the Alps. They began their test on 20 June and completed it on 31 August.

In June and July of 2007, the Army Air Corps balloon travelled to the Italian Alps to fly in the daunting environment of the Mondovi Valley. The balloon was flown by fifteen AAC personnel, gaining balloon flying experience to rival that of the bold aviators of the late nineteenth century who first took the British Army into the air.

Over one hundred members of the Army Air Corps, drawn

ABOVE AND LEFT: PROJECTS UNDERTAKEN TO CELEBRATE THE GOLDEN JUBILEE INCLUDED AAC BALLOON FLIGHTS IN THE MONDOVI VALLEY, THE ALPS 4000 CHALLENGE AND EXERCISE GOLDEN EAGLE.

from all of the units across the Corps, trained for public duties that were to be undertaken in April and May. The Army Air Corps Queen's Guard Squadron, supported by the Army Air Corps Band were highly praised for their turnout and the execution of their drill when they provided the Royal Guard at Buckingham Palace, St James's Palace, the Tower of London and Windsor Castle. A detachment was also deployed to Scotland to provide the Royal Guard at Holyrood House.

The main official celebration event to mark the Golden Jubilee took place on 15 September 2007 at Middle Wallop. Scores of vintage aircraft, the majority of which were trusty old Austers, flew in to the airfield early in the morning to form a static display parked behind vintage armoured vehicles and the various helicopter types flown by the AAC over the years. This gave the hundreds of arriving guests a tremendous view as they took morning coffee in the sunshine prior to the commencement of the day's events.

His Royal Highness the Prince of Wales, Colonel-in-Chief of the Army Air Corps for the last fifteen years, was in attendance for the dedication of the AAC Memorial which culminated in a fly past of AAC aircraft led by the Auster, Chipmunk, Sioux, Scout and Alouette of the Corps' own Historic Aircraft Flight. This was followed by a parade at midday when His Royal Highness gave a speech in which he described the preceding fifty years as having been '. . . an extraordinary period that has seen enormous leaps in technology, and operations that have spanned the globe. It has seen the Corps' stock continue to rise across Defence and it now sits firmly at the heart of the British Army and is a vital component of almost every operation.'

The main purpose of the parade was for the trooping of the AAC Guidon. His Royal Highness had presented the Guidon (a heraldic banner of the type once carried into battle by cavalry regiments to form a rallying point for the troops) to the Corps in 1994. At that time the Guidon had the AAC badge at its centre, its monogram in two of the four corners and, to honour their part in the creation of the Corps, the badges of the Glider Pilot Regiment and the Royal Regiment of Artillery in the other two. It also bore the two Theatre Honours awarded to the AAC – 'Falkland Islands 1982' and 'Gulf 1991'. Added to the Guidon since then were the further Honours 'Iraq 2003', 'Wadi Al Batin', and 'Al Basra'. In the AAC's Golden Jubilee year, Her Majesty The Queen graciously

ABOVE: THE AAC QUEEN'S GUARD SQUADRON PERFORMED ITS FIRST PUBLIC DUTIES AT BUCKINGHAM PALACE IN MAY 2007.

allowed the Corps to emblazon the Honours of its predecessor, the Glider Pilot Regiment – 'Landing in Sicily', 'Sicily 1943', 'Southern France', 'Pegasus Bridge', 'Merville Battery', 'Normandy Landing', 'Arnhem', 'Rhine' and 'NW Europe 1944-45'. The Guidon now proudly carries fourteen Battle and Theatre Honours.

While Prince Charles paid warm tribute to the soldiers of the AAC and those who have gone before them, so too did many others. The Red Arrows staged a fly-past over the parade ground as a salute to the AAC and later a Lancaster, Hurricane and Spitfire of the Battle of Britain Memorial Flight, celebrating their own sixty-seventh birthday on Battle of Britain Day, delighted the crowd with a tremendous display. The Blue Eagles amazed the crowd by

BELOW: THERE WAS A DEDICATION CEREMONY FOR THE NEW AAC MEMORIAL WALL AT MIDDLE WALLOP ON 15 SEPTEMBER 2007.

ABOVE: HIS ROYAL HIGHNESS, THE PRINCE OF WALES INSPECTS THE PARADE FOR THE TROOPING OF THE NEW AAC GUIDON AT MIDDLE WALLOP ON 15 SEPTEMBER 2007.

RIGHT: THE AAC MEMORIAL WINDOW (OR LIGHT) IN SALISBURY CATHEDRAL, WHICH PORTRAYS THE AAC COLLECT ON ONE SIDE AND THE FAMOUS QUOTE FROM ISIAH CHAPTER 48 VERSE 31 ON THE OTHER, WAS DESIGNED AND PAINTED BY THE ARTIST CAROLINE SWASH.

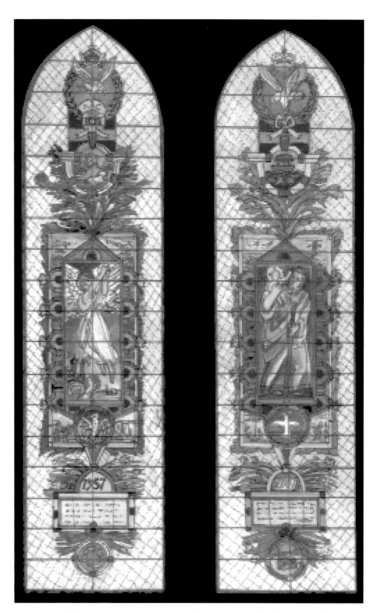

twisting, turning, flipping and rolling helicopters in ways that only they can do, the Red Devils dropped in in spectacular style and there was a truly breathtaking glider-and-tug aerobatic display in tribute to the GPR. Further fly-pasts, displays and massed formations of helicopters continued into the early evening as the weather remained gloriously sunny. It was a perfect day for a party.

The Golden Jubilee provided an ideal opportunity to review the history of the Corps and the great achievements of the men and women who have served with the Army Air Corps, the Glider Pilot Regiment, the Air Observation Post, the Royal Flying Corps, the Royal Engineers, the Royal Artillery and every other organisation, military and civilian, that has been in some way responsible for

putting soldiers in the air. Many lessons can be learned from the past. The Army Air Corps has developed into a formidable fighting force whose participation in offensive operations today is often deemed essential to their success. Past experience shows that the continued success of the Corps in the future will rely very much on its well-practised ability to evolve, changing to suit the ever-changing circumstances in which it must operate and adapting to the demands of ever more sophisticated technology.

There is little doubt that in the future the process of change will have to be handled more efficiently and more swiftly as the nature of the work undertaken by the AAC demands that the Corps becomes ever more versatile. The break-up of the Soviet Union has meant that the AAC no longer needs to train to stem the advance of the Warsaw Pact forces in Germany. Training has been, and will continue to be, adapted to suit operations elsewhere. Operation Banner in Northern Ireland came to an end in 2007 and 5 Regiment's activities have been substantially scaled down but that does not mean to say that the Corps no longer has a role to play in the UK. The creation of 6 Regiment AAC (V), based at Bury St Edmunds, to join the Netheravon-based territorial unit 7 Regiment (which also has flights operating from RAF Shawbury and RAF Leuchars), demonstrates the importance of Army flying at home. Not only do the territorial units train personnel to provide reinforcements for the regular AAC regiments, but they are also heavily involved in what are referred to as 'civil contingencies'. For 7 Regiment that meant

helping out with relief and support operations during the severe flooding in the UK during 2007, or controlling and managing the airspace around Gleneagles during the G8 Summit in 2005. While the territorial units do not have aircraft on permanent standby for emergencies, they can have a Gazelle airborne within minutes if needs be.

The AAC will also, of course, continue to fly wherever the British Army is required to operate. Whatever the challenge they face, the men and women of today's Army Air Corps, with half a century of experience behind them, can be relied upon to meet it head on. Their expertise and versatility will ensure that, when the AAC comes to celebrate its Centenary in fifty years' time, it will be able to look back over another half-century of amazing achievement.

THE NEW AAC GUIDON, WHICH NOW CARRIES FOURTEEN BATTLE AND THEATRE HONOURS.